Face of the Nation 1987

Statistical Supplement to the 18th Edition of the
Encyclopedia of Social Work

Sumner M. Rosen, David Fanshel, and Mary E. Lutz, Editors

National Association of Social Workers
Silver Spring, Maryland

Face of the nation, 1987.

    1. Social service—United States—Statistics.
2. United States—Population—Statistics.   I. Rosen,
Sumner M.   II. Fanshel, David.   III. Lutz, Mary E.
IV. National Association of Social Workers.
HV90.F33 1987   361′.973   86-18219
ISBN 0-87101-142-5

Printed in U.S.A.

Designer: Steffie Kaplan

CONTENTS

ACKNOWLEDGMENTS

Federal government agencies whose work we found helpful, although we did not always cite it, include the Federal Reserve Board, the National Center for Health Statistics, the Centers for Disease Control, the Social Security Administration, the Office of Management and Budget, the Immigration and Naturalization Service, and the Bureau of Labor Statistics. People in search of statistical information will find the publications of these agencies useful. The regional office of the U.S. Bureau of the Census in New York City provided helpful information, as did the regional office of the Bureau of Labor Statistics. For information in the section on child welfare we are indebted to Dr. Charles P. Gershenson of the Administration for Children, Youth, and Families (Department of Health and Human Services).

Individuals who provided advice, feedback, and links to others include Victor W. Sidel, Tom Joe, Bahrend A. DeVries, Cushing Dolbeare, Richard Michel, Wendell Primus, Sheldon Danziger, Kim Smeeding, and Robert Bonn. Allen Rubin provided much of the information in the section on social work education. *The State of Black America, 1986*, published by the National Urban League, contains much valuable information and insights. Andrew Hacker's continuing creative use of statistics has been an important stimulus.

Columbia University colleagues who were helpful include George Brager, Peter Marcuse, Robb Burlage, Saskia Sassen-Koob, Kim Hopper, Howard Berliner, and Alfred J. Kahn. At the NASW Publications Office we worked closely and harmoniously with Jacqueline Atkins and Kenneth Greenhall, whose support we are glad to acknowledge. Maurice Matiz produced many of the graphic illustrations; Sylvia Shultz did the word processing of the tables and text.

We wish to acknowledge the generous financial support of the New World Foundation.

SUMNER M. ROSEN
DAVID FANSHEL
MARY E. LUTZ

INTRODUCTION

Face of the Nation is a wide-ranging statistical supplement to the eighteenth edition of the *Encyclopedia of Social Work*. The information presented is as up to date as possible and draws on a broad spectrum of sources. The criteria we believe should govern a work of this nature and that we have tried to put into practice include the following:

1. That the work provides access to a wide range of data that would normally require extensive searching in places and among sources not readily available to students, teachers, practitioners, or other users.

2. That the data—chosen from a wide range of possible inclusion—are relevant and useful to teachers, students, and practitioners of social policy and social welfare; also, that the material is of interest and use to wider groups of scholars, analysts, and advocates—particularly, that it provides information enabling users to make the connections that help them to understand, describe, and specify particular issues and trends.

3. That the material gives visible form to the idea that "statistics are people with the tears washed off"[1] and that it makes clear—whatever the level of abstraction or generality presented by a table or graph—that human beings are our real concern.

4. That the format of the tables and graphs and the accompanying captions make the meaning we see as clear as possible; numbers can tell us much about real life, and we should not permit ourselves to be put off by them.

5. That the sources used are documented as fully as necessary to enable users to find more than we were able to include.

Data are included that provide an overall view of particular areas of interest and concern, and many of the tables have been disaggregated in an attempt to illuminate the underlying reality. The question that guided us in doing this was: How well or poorly does our society create and distribute wealth and income, allocate resources to meet social and communal needs, and enable people to adjust to changes in economic and social structures

and processes? Our test of any process or outcome is how well it protects the weak and the vulnerable, heals the sick, sustains the well, provides jobs and income, cares for the aged, and provides for the poor, the institutionalized, and others who cannot provide for themselves.

Because of our awareness of the crucial role played by economic forces in determining social outcomes, we cover some key economic issues. In part, our cue comes from the pastoral letter on the economy issued in 1986 by the National Conference of Catholic Bishops, which asks what our economy does for and to people—precisely the right tests to apply. Increasingly, we see how deeply and directly the social welfare enterprise is shaped by economic, demographic, ideological, and other contextual forces. Our selection of topics and content was guided by our view that causes and consequences need to be connected and made as clear as possible. The issues raised in the pastoral letter will attract wider attention in the years to come; we want our readers to be well equipped to take part in the discussion that has already begun.

Assembling a volume of this kind involves more than simply extracting tables from standard sources. It is necessary to determine how accurate figures are, how valid they are as reflections of reality, what degree of confidence to repose in them and how best to convey complicated, often sensitive issues in quantitative form. Where possible, we provide data that track information over time to help users see trends.

Each of the substantive sections has its own introduction. These provide a framework for the graphs and tables, with interpretive comments intended to help readers understand the concerns that guided our selections and to know something about the thoughts and reflections of those who put this material together. In some cases, they also provide information of interest that could not be included in the text because of limitations of space.

We dealt with a wide range of resources, among which three kinds stand out: (1) official government agencies that gather, analyze, and disseminate data; (2) groups that

---

[1] V. W. Sidel, MD (1986). "Presidential Address to the American Public Health Association, November, 1985." *APHA Journal,* 76(4), 374.

advocate for the welfare of particular populations; and (3) research organizations.

Having said that our work is as up to date as we could make it, we must also say that budget cuts and personnel reductions in federal statistical agencies have limited the amount and level of information available. We nevertheless affirm that, in every case, the federal officials whose help we sought gave it readily and gracefully.

We want to record our deep appreciation to all those who provided data, led us to the right source, and helped us to understand and judge the relevance and reliability of the material we considered. Without exception the organizations and individuals to whom we turned were responsive and cooperative. We want to express our particular appreciation to the officials in the U.S. Bureau of the Census who provided us with several of the graphs and charts that are included; they add to the usefulness and visual quality of this volume. From all who use this work we welcome comments and suggestions that will make future revisions more helpful and more fully related to the needs of the users. The "Statistical and Demographic Trends" section of the 1983-84 supplement to the seventeenth edition of the *Encyclopedia of Social Work* was the work of Sumner M. Rosen and David Fanshel. The present work involved the participation of a third author, Mary E. Lutz.

We are aware that we are on a path opened by earlier gatherers of information: Grace and Edith Abbott, Sophonisba Breckinridge, Bradley Buell, Paul Kellogg, Paul Schreiber, Mary Van Kleeck, and many others. How they would envy us the computerized databases, computer graphics, and other technologies of the current period! What they lacked in data-processing capability, however, they made up in their social vision. We conceived of our work in the spirit of these pioneers.

We greatly appreciate the opportunity made available to us by NASW to embark on this venture. The decision to add a third volume—devoted to statistical information of the kind presented here—to the eighteenth edition of the *Encyclopedia of Social Work* reflects an impressive commitment of publishing resources to the mission of social work. We know of no other professional association that has made this kind of major investment in the organization of social information. For those who are new to the ranks of service professions such as social work, we hope the availability of important information about societal trends will whet their appetites for enriched social perspectives. For the many direct service practitioners who make up the vast majority of the more than 100,000 members of NASW, we hope that in the course of ministering to the needs of the many distressed persons, families, and communities who seek their help, they will make a special effort to understand the larger social context in which their clients' problems developed. In the spirit of René Dubos we urge: "Act locally, think globally."

Sources

The tables and graphics have individual source notes fully documenting the material covered. Because the introductions to the 11 sections present a wealth of data in concentrated form, however, it was felt that the inclusion of specific reference citations would prove distracting to users of this volume. What follows, therefore—unless otherwise noted in the introductions themselves—is a listing of our principal sources, drawn from official government agencies, advocacy groups, research organizations, and commercial publications: the Center for Budget and Policy Priorities; the Children's Defense Fund; Citizens for Tax Justice; the Federal Reserve Board; *Forbes* magazine; *Fortune* magazine; the Institute for Research on Poverty of the University of Wisconsin; the Institute for Socioeconomic Studies the National Center for Health Statistics; the National Conference of State Legislatures; the National Housing Conference; the National Institute of Mental Health; the *New York Times;* the Organization for Economic Cooperation and Development; the Population Reference Bureau; the Urban Institute; the U.S. Bureau of the Census; the U.S. General Accounting Office; and the Committee on Ways and Means of the U.S. House of Representatives.

SUMNER M. ROSEN
DAVID FANSHEL
MARY E. LUTZ

SECTION 1. U.S. DEMOGRAPHIC CHARACTERISTICS

The U.S. population grew by 4.2 percent between 1980 and 1984, the nonwhite population growing faster than the white. Geographic growth was uneven. The South and West accounted for 91 percent of total population growth between 1980 and 1985. The population grew by 2 million or more in California, Texas, and Florida. The latter two, plus Alaska, Nevada, Utah, and Arizona, showed growth of 10 percent or more. Fifteen metropolitan areas grew by more than 15 percent each, and 15 shrank by 2 to 5 percent each. Growth was most marked in Texas and Florida, decline greatest in Michigan and Indiana. Population fell between 1970 and 1980 in 12 large cities: New York, Chicago, Philadelphia, Detroit, Baltimore, Indianapolis, Washington, Milwaukee, Cleveland, Boston, San Francisco, and New Orleans. The number of foreign-born residents reached new postwar highs.

The United States remains an urban-suburban nation; 76 percent of the population live in metropolitan areas, down less than 1 percent from 1970. The six largest cities with populations of a million or more contained 17.7 million people in 1984. One hundred seventy-six cities had populations of 100,000 or more; 30.7 million people lived in the 25 largest cities. Between 1970 and 1980 the population grew faster and incomes rose more in suburbs than in cities. In 1970, blacks constituted a majority in Atlanta and in the District of Columbia; by 1980 they were a majority in Detroit, Baltimore, and New Orleans. Blacks, Hispanics, and other nonwhite groups together constituted majorities in Chicago, Houston, and Los Angeles. Slowed growth of blacks in cities and some movement to the suburbs was outweighed by continued white exodus from cities to suburbs. The rapidly growing Hispanic population is largely concentrated in 10 of the 305 metropolitan areas; almost half live in these areas, with large concentrations in New York and Los Angeles. In each of the last three census years—1960, 1970, 1980—Florida and California showed the highest immigration of people 65 and above from other states.

By 1984, one in four families with children was a single-parent family: 20 percent of white children and 59 percent of black children lived in single-parent families, compared with 1970 figures of 10 percent and 36 percent. These are one aspect of the dramatic changes occurring in family structure, reflected also in increasing numbers of female-headed households and higher numbers of babies born to unmarried mothers—currently more than 20 percent of all births. In 1982, 15 percent of white and 47 percent of black mothers were single parents, compared with 8 percent and 31 percent in 1970. Divorce and absence of spouse accounted for 81 percent of white single mothers; 69 percent of black single mothers were in the "never married" and "absent spouse" categories. In 1982, 10 percent of white and 41 percent of black single mothers were "never married"; in 1970 these figures were 3 percent and 18 percent. More than two-thirds of nonwhite women aged 20–24 were single in 1980, compared with one-third in 1965. Separation rates for married women have been six to seven times higher among nonwhite than among white women. The median age of marriage has risen slowly since 1960.

Marriage and divorce rates have been relatively stable since the late 1970s. Most children still live in two-parent families, but the share is smaller than ever; single-person and nonfamily households reached new high levels in 1984, as did the share of single and divorced people in the adult population. More mothers of children of all ages are in the labor force than ever before. The share of people 65 and over also continued to grow; this should continue with increasing life expectancies. In part as a result of these trends, in 1984 average household size reached a new low—2.69 people.

The number of immigrants rose, and their distribution by geographic origin shifted. The number of undocumented immigrants is not known; best estimates of the number in the United States as of 1986 range from 2.1 to 2.4 million—about half from Mexico—largely concentrated in California and seven other states. Foreign-born people constituted a majority of the population of Miami and were one-fifth or more in San Francisco, Los Angeles, and New York.

Changes in the ethnic and national mix of our population, family structure, and where people live and will live all exert their influence on the social process, social policy issues, and the response society makes.

TABLE 1.1. POPULATION OF THE UNITED STATES, 1790–1980, WITH PROJECTIONS TO 2000
(IN THOUSANDS)

In 1985 nonwhites were 14.9 percent of the total—the highest proportion since 1850—and their representation was expected to continue to increase. Total population more than doubled since 1920 and was almost double the 1930 level in 1985.

Year	Total Population Residing in U.S.	Number White	Number Nonwhite[a]	Percentage White
1790	3,929	3,172	757	80.7
1800	5,308	4,306	1,002	81.1
1810	7,240	5,862	1,378	81.0
1920	9,638	7,867	1,771	81.6
1830	12,866	10,537	2,329	81.9
1840	17,069	14,196	2,874	83.2
1850	23,192	19,553	3,639	84.3
1860	31,443	26,923	4,521	85.6
1870[b]	39,818	34,337	5,481	86.2
1880	50,156	43,403	6,753	86.5
1890	62,948	55,101	7,846	87.5
1900	75,995	66,809	9,185	87.9
1910	91,972	81,732	10,240	88.9
1920	105,711	94,821	10,890	89.7
1930	122,775	110,287	12,488	89.8
1940	131,669	118,215	13,454	89.8
1950	151,326	134,942	15,755	89.2
1960[c]	179,323	158,832	20,492	88.6
1970	203,302	178,098	25,138	87.6
1980	226,546	194,779	31,833	85.9
1985	238,631	203,113	29,074	85.1
1990[d]	249,657	210,790	31,412	84.4
2000[d]	267,955	222,654	35,733	83.1

[a]1790–1850, black only.
[b]Revised to include adjustments for undernumeration in southern states.
[c]Beginning in 1950, figures include Alaska and Hawaii.
[d]Projections assume that women entering childbearing age will have an average of 1.9 births, net immigration will be 450,000 per year, and the mortality rate will improve slightly.
Source: U.S. Bureau of the Census, *Statistical Abstract of the United States, 1986* (Washington, D.C.: U.S. Government Printing Office, 1986), p. 25.

TABLE 1.2 HOUSEHOLDS,[a] FAMILIES, MARITAL STATUS, AND LIVING ARRANGEMENTS—CHANGES, 1970–1985

Between 1970 and 1985, total households rose by 37 percent, family households by 22 percent, and nonfamily households by 102 percent. Fifty-two percent of all new households formed in that period were nonfamily households. The percentage of children living in other than married-couple families doubled from 11.1 percent in 1970 to 22.2 percent in 1985.

Category	Number of Households (in thousands)			Percentage of Population		
	1970	1980	1985	1970	1980	1985
Total number households	63,401	80,776	86,789	100.0	100.0	100.0
Average persons per household[b]	3.14	2.76	2.69			
Family households	51,456	59,550	62,706	81.2	73.7	72.3
Married-couple family	44,728	49,112	50,350	70.5	60.8	58.0
Children under 18	25,532	24,961	24,210	—	—	—
Other family, female householder	5,500	8,705	10,129	8.7	10.8	11.7
Children under 18	2,858	5,445	6,006	—	—	—
Other family, male householder	1,228	1,733	2,228	1.9	2.1	2.6
Children under 18	341	616	896	—	—	—
Nonfamily households	11,945	21,226	24,082	18.8	26.3	27.7
Male householder	4,063	8,807	10,114	6.4	10.9	11.7
Living alone	3,532	6,966	7,922			
Female householder	7,882	12,419	13,968	12.4	15.4	16.1
Living alone	7,349	11,330	12,680			

[a]Family households consist of two or more persons related by marriage, blood, or adoption; "other" families are those with no spouse present. The householder, in general, is the adult financially responsible for the household.

[b]Numbers not in thousands.

Sources: U.S. Bureau of the Census, "Population Profile of the United States, 1983–84," in *Current Population Reports* (Series P-23, No. 14, Washington, D.C.: U.S. Government Printing Office, 1984), pp. 38–39; and "Households, Families, Marital Status and Living Arrangements: March 1985," in *Current Population Reports* (Series P-20, No. 402), p. 7.

TABLE 1.3. BIRTHRATES BY RACE, 1950–1983; ESTIMATED NUMBER AND RATES OF BIRTHS TO UNMARRIED WOMEN, 1950–1983

Birthrates for married women peaked between 1955 and 1960. Differences by race were relatively stable and moved consistently except for a sharper decline among nonwhite than white teenagers between 1965 and 1980. Differences in birthrates were stable over much of the 1950–1980 period and showed similar rates of decline after the peak rates of 1955–1960.

| Year | Total Live Births[a] (in thousands) | Rate per 1,000 Population | | | Births to Unmarried Women | | | |
| | | | | | Total (in thousands) | Rate per 1,000 Unmarried Women[b] | | |
		Total	White	Black and Other		Rate	White	Black and Other
1950	3,632	24.1	23.3	33.3	141.6	14.1	6.1	71.2
1955	4,097	25.0	23.8	34.5	183.3	19.3	7.9	87.2
1960	4,258	23.7	22.7	32.1	224.3	21.6	9.2	98.3
1965	3,760	19.4	18.3	27.6	291.2	23.5	11.6	97.6
1970	3,731	18.4	17.4	25.1[c]	398.7	26.4	13.8	89.9
1975	3,144	14.6	13.6	21.0	447.9	24.5	12.4	79.0
1976	3,168	14.8	13.6	20.8	468.1	24.3	12.6	76.4
1977	3,327	15.4	14.1	21.6	515.7	25.6	13.5	77.4
1978	3,333	15.0	14.0	21.6	543.9	25.7	13.7	76.5
1979	3,474	15.6	14.5	22.2	597.8	27.2	14.9	78.2
1980	3,612	15.9	14.9	22.5	665.7	29.4	17.6	77.2
1981	3,629	15.8	14.8	22.0	686.6	29.6	18.2	75.4
1982	3,681	15.9	14.9	21.9	715.2	30.0	18.8	73.9
1983	3,639	15.5	14.6	21.3	—	—	—	—

[a]Through 1955, adjusted for underregistration.   [c]1971.
[b]Never married, widowed, or divorced.
Sources: U.S. Bureau of the Census, *Statistical Abstract of the United States, 1985* (Washington, D.C.: U.S. Government Printing Office, 1984), pp. 58, 59, 64; and *Statistical Abstract of the United States, 1986*, pp. 57, 62.

TABLE 1.4. LEGAL ABORTIONS—ESTIMATED NUMBER, RATE, AND RATIO BY RACE—1972–1981 (WOMEN 15–44 YEARS OLD)

Abortion rose more in the 1970s than in the 1980s. Abortion rates were stable for black women and declined for white women in the early 1980s.

| | White | | Black and Other | | |
	Number of Abortions (in thousands)	Abortion Rate per 1,000 Women	Number of Abortions (in thousands)	Abortion Rate per 1,000 Women	Ratio of Black and Other to White Rate
1972	455.3	11.8	131.5	21.7	1.8
1975	701.2	17.2	333.0	49.3	2.9
1976	784.9	18.8	394.4	56.3	3.0
1977	888.8	20.9	427.9	59.0	2.8
1978	969.4	22.3	440.2	58.7	2.6
1979	1,062.4	24.0	435.3	56.2	2.3
1980	1,093.6	24.3	460.3	56.8	2.3
1981	1,107.8	24.3	469.6	55.9	2.3

Source: *Statistical Abstract of the United States, 1985*, p. 67.

FIGURE 1.1. LIVING ARRANGEMENTS OF CHILDREN, BY RACE, 1984

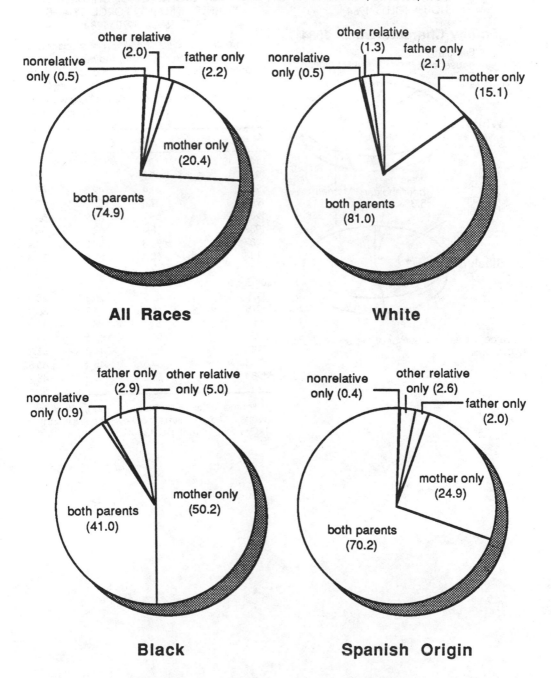

Source: Data from U.S. Bureau of the Census, "Population Profile of the United States, 1983–84," in *Current Population Reports* (Series P-23, No. 14, Washington, D.C.: U.S. Government Printing Office, 1984).

FIGURE 1.2 CHARACTERISTICS OF HOUSEHOLDS, 1984

Family Characteristics: 1984

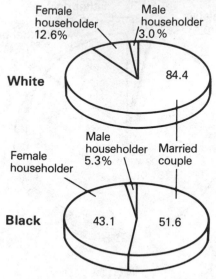

White

Female householder 12.6%

Male householder 3.0%

84.4

Black

Female householder

Male householder 5.3%

Married couple

43.1   51.6

Source: *Statistical Abstract of the United States, 1986,* p. xviii.

TABLE 1.5. PERCENTAGE OF CHILDREN WITH MOTHERS IN LABOR FORCE, BY AGE AND RACE, 1970–1984

Substantial numbers of children of all ages are the children of working mothers. The increase in the representation of employed mothers of young children is particularly striking. More black than white mothers work, but the differences narrowed over this period.

Age and Year	Black	White	Total
Under 18			
1970	49.2	37.1	38.8
1975	51.4	42.8	44.0
1980	57.4	52.0	52.8
1981	58.7	52.9	54.5
1982	58.4	54.2	54.9
1983	58.8	54.2	54.9
1984	60.4	55.8	56.3
Under 6			
1970	42.9	26.3	28.5
1975	48.4	34.2	35.9
1980	51.4	41.7	43.0
1981	53.0	43.6	44.9
1982	52.9	44.8	45.8
1983	54.6	45.4	46.8
1984	55.0	47.3	48.2

Source: Children's Defense Fund, *Black and White Children in America: Key Facts* (Washington, D.C.: Author, 1985), pp. 124–125.

TABLE 1.6. PERSONS BELOW POVERTY BY SELECTED CHARACTERISTICS, 1975–1984[a]

Poverty rates increased in this period for all groups shown except people over 65.

Categories and Years	Total Persons	Age 65 and Over	In Families Total Persons	In Families Related Children Under 18
All Groups				
1984	33,700	3,330	26,458	12,929
Rate	14.4	12.4	13.1	21.0
1980	29,272	3,871	22,601	11,114
Rate	13.0	15.7	11.5	17.9
1975	25,877	3,317	20,789	10,882
Rate	12.3	15.3	10.9	16.8
White				
1984	22,955	2,579	17,299	8.086
Rate	11.5	10.7	10.1	16.1
1980	19,699	3,042	14,587	6,817
Rate	10.2	13.6	8.6	13.4
1975	17,770	2,634	13,799	6,748
Rate	9.7	13.4	8.3	12.5
Black				
1984	9,490	710	8,104	4,320
Rate	33.8	31.7	32.2	46.2
1980	8,579	783	7,190	3,906
Rate	32.5	38.1	31.1	42.1
1975	7,545	652	6,533	3,884
Rate	31.3	36.3	30.1	41.4
Hispanic[b]				
1984	4,806	176	4,192	2,317
Rate	28.4	21.5	27.4	38.7
1980	3,491	179	3,143	1,718
Rate	25.7	30.8	25.1	33.0
1975	2,991	137	2,755	1,619
Rate	26.9	32.6	26.3	33.1

[a]Numbers in thousands.
[b]Hispanic persons may be of any race. Therefore rates and numbers do not sum to totals.
Source: U.S. Bureau of the Census, "Money, Income and Poverty Status of Families and Persons in the United States—1984," in *Current Population Reports* (Series P-60, No. 149), p. 21.

TABLE 1.7. NUMBER OF PERSONS AND PROPORTIONS OF THE POPULATION 65 YEARS OF AGE
OR OVER AND 75 YEARS OF AGE OR OVER—SELECTED YEARS, 1960–1990   (IN THOUSANDS)

People over 65 and 75 increased to new highs; this trend is expected to continue.

Year	65 Years or Over		75 Years or Over	
	Number	Percentage	Number	Percentage
Historical				
1960	17,147	9.1	5,775	3.1
1965	18,952	9.3	6,879	3.4
1970	20,681	9.7	8,133	3.8
1975	23,309	10.4	9,308	4.1
1980	26,364	11.2	10,585	4.5
1981	26,928	11.3	10,900	4.6
1982	27,503	11.4	11,238	4.7
1983	28,078	11.5	11,558	4.8
Projections				
1985	29,319	11.8	12,226	4.9
1988	31,325	12.3	13,325	5.2
1990	32,570	12.6	14,054	5.4

Source: U.S. Department of Health and Human Services, *Health Care Financing Review,* 6(3)
(Washington, D.C.: Author, 1985), p. 4.

TABLE 1.8. PERCENTAGE OF THE POPULATION MARRIED AND DIVORCED,
18 YEARS AND OVER, 1960–1984

*The percentage of married women decreased among all age groups between 1960 and 1984,
more among blacks than whites. By 1984, 44.5 percent of all black women
were married. Divorce rates rose among all groups shown. Marriages rose substantially
among both men and women between 1971 and 1981.*

Sex and Race	1960	1965	1970	1975	1980	1983	1984
Percentage married							
Male	76.4	76.2	75.3	72.8	68.4	66.6	65.8
White	77.3	76.9	74.9	70.7	69.6	68.3	67.7
Black and other	68.4	70.2	63.1	57.5	55.2	52.2	50.6[a]
Female	71.6	70.5	68.5	66.7	63.0	61.4	60.8
White	72.2	70.9	68.8	65.2	64.1	63.3	62.8
Black and other	66.3	67.6	58.9	51.8	50.9	45.7	44.5[a]
Percentage divorced							
Male	2.0	2.5	2.5	3.7	5.2	5.8	6.1
White	2.0	2.4	3.3	4.5	5.5	5.7	6.0
Black and other	2.2	2.4	4.8	6.6	7.0	7.4	7.0[a]
Female	2.9	3.3	3.9	5.3	7.1	7.9	8.3
White	2.7	3.1	4.7	6.4	7.2	7.6	8.0
Black and other	4.8	4.5	6.3	8.3	9.6	10.5	11.0[a]

[a]Black only.
Sources: *Statistical Abstract of the United States, 1982–83,* p. 41; and *Statistical Abstract of the United
States, 1986,* p. 35.

FIGURE 1.3. U.S. IMMIGRATION PATTERNS, BY REGION OF ORIGIN, 1945–1985 (PERCENTAGE)

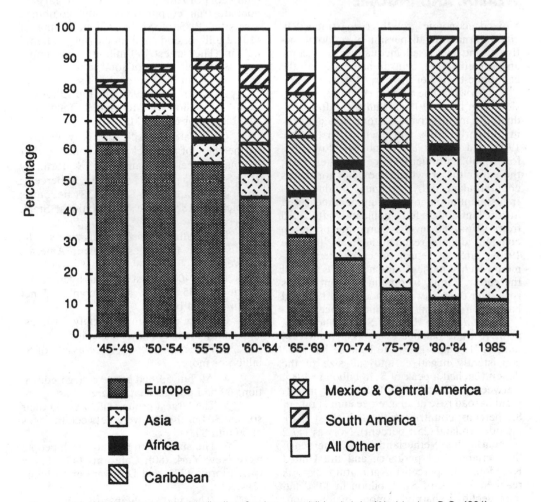

Source: U.S. Immigration and Naturalization Service, unpublished data (Washington, D.C., 1986).

SECTION 2. THE ECONOMY, WEALTH, AND INCOME

Slowed economic growth, rising trade deficits, international dispersion of economic activity, and increased inequalities in income and wealth were central hallmarks of the economic trends of the early 1980s.

Growth. The rate of economic growth slowed in the mid-1970s and thereafter. Productivity in the private sector reached a peak in the early 1960s and declined in the late 1970s and early 1980s to postwar lows. Before 1980, productivity per worker rose; thereafter the growth in the labor force was counterbalanced by declining productivity. Investment in plant and equipment measured in constant dollars fell significantly after 1980 from 1976–1980 levels. Corporate profits in constant dollars reached highs in the late 1970s; rates of return on corporate investment reached highes in the mid-1960s and fell thereafter. Family income in constant dollars rose over the postwar decades until 1979 and have been stagnant or declining since then.

Trade. The United States showed a positive trade balance every year from 1894 until 1971. Since 1977, the balance has been consistently negative, and the size of the deficit reached a peak of $118 billion in 1985. Between 1977 and 1982 U.S. direct investment abroad rose at an average annual rate of 8.7 percent; countries with the highest share included Ireland (25.5 percent), Norway (17.2 percent), the Netherlands (14.2 percent), Switzerland (13.1 percent), and the United Kingdom (13.1 percent). Agricultural exports reached a peak of $43.8 billion in 1981 and then declined sharply. Among major manufactured products the level of domestic sales represented by imports ranged from 0 to 11 percent in the 1950–1975 period; by 1983 the range was 15 to 80 percent, including shoes (65 percent), textile machinery (50 percent), TV sets and radios (60 percent), machine tools (36 percent), cars (27 percent), and steel (22 percent).

Inequalities and Dominance. If countries ranked by the size of their GNP were compared with corporations ranked by level of sales (based on 1978 figures), the largest 50 entities would include General Motors, Exxon, Ford, Royal Dutch/Shell, Mobil, Texaco, British Petroleum, and Standard Oil of California. In 1986, according to *Fortune* magazine's analyses, the 500 largest industrial corporations and the 500 largest nonindustrial corporations show combined assets in 1985 of $1.91 trillion, profits of $107.2 billion, and total employment of 15.5 million. The largest 100 military contractors increased their share of total military prime contracts from 65.9 percent in fiscal 1982 to 70.1 percent in fiscal 1985; the top 12 ranged from $8.9 billion for McDonnell Douglas to $2.7 billion for Martin Marietta.

Corporate diversification is symbolized by the share of nonsteel assets owned in 1981 by major steel companies: USX (formerly U.S. Steel), 65 percent; ARMCO, 54 percent; Jones & Laughlin-LTV, 33 percent; Bethlehem, 18 percent; and National Steel, 14 percent.

Highlights of *Forbes* magazine's 1985 figures on the 400 richest people in America showed that:

1. The 400 richest have an average net worth of $335 million and a combined net worth of $134 billion.

2. There are 77 major family fortunes, with many members among the 400.

3. Fifteen of the 400 have assets of $1 billion or more.

4. All but 50 had some college education; 69 had postgraduate degrees.

5. The largest group (119) were in their sixties; 304 of the 400 were between the ages of 50 and 80.

6. The states with the most rich people were New York (80), California (49), Texas (44), Florida (23), and Delaware and Illinois (21 each).

7. The metropolitan areas with the most rich people were New York (81), Dallas/Fort Worth (25), Los Angeles (23), and Chicago and Wilmington (21 each).

8. Colleges with large numbers of rich alumni include Yale (25), Harvard (12), MIT (10), Princeton (9), and NYU and Stanford (8 each).

9. The most important sources of wealth are banking and finance (25), New York real estate (32), retailing (19), and high technology (12).

A March 1986 analysis of wealthy families in the *Federal Reserve Bulletin* reported that .05 percent of all families had incomes above $280,000. Almost all are Caucasian; the largest share (31 percent) work in banking, insurance, and real estate. More than 80 percent—higher among those aged 65 and above and among those with inherited wealth—had $1 million or more in net worth, with an average value of $5.4 million. The top 10 percent of income receivers owned 85 percent of publicly traded stock, 92 percent of municipal bonds, 72 percent of all other bonds, 80 percent of mutual funds, and 88 percent of trust accounts owned by families. Families in the top 1 percent of the income distribution held 19 percent of all assets and 34 percent of financial assets.

Since the 1930s the number of farms has fallen from 6.3 million to 2.3 million. The largest 1.3 percent of farms, measured by gross income, account for 29 percent of all farm revenues; small farms represent 72 percent of the total but only 13 percent of sales. Farm income in 1983 was $16.1 billion, half the total five years earlier and the lowest since 1971. Total farm income in 1983 in constant dollars was the lowest since the 1930s. Total farm debt rose from $80 billion in 1974 to $214 billion in 1984.

Between 1979 and 1982 the number of people officially measured as poor increased by 9.9 million, or 40 percent. One estimate is that the 1981–1982 recession added 1.6 million persons to the poverty rolls, and the 1981 budget and legislative changes an additional 557,000. In 1965, the official poverty line was 46 percent of median income; by 1968 it had fallen to 41 percent. Between 1972 and 1980 it was in the 38–40 percent range, and by 1982 it had reached 42 percent.

Between 1960 and 1981 the number of poor people in male-headed families decreased by 50 percent; it rose by 54 percent among female-headed families. Female-headed families are about five times more likely to be poor than married-couple families. In 1983, 13.8 million children were counted as poor—22 percent of all children under 18. They represented almost 40 percent of all the poor, the highest rate among children since the early 1960s. Between 1968 and 1983, whereas the total number of children decreased by 9 million, the number of poor children rose by 3 million. By contrast, more than one-third of all people 65 and above were poor in 1959; this had fallen to 14.6 percent by 1984.

Among older people poverty is higher among women living alone than among other women. About one older person in four is "near poor," with an income at or below 126 percent of the poverty level. In 1950, earnings provided almost half the income of older people as against 23 percent in 1978. For two-thirds of those 65 and over, social security provides half or more of their income; for 26 percent it provides 90 percent or more. Widows and women over 75 who retired early show higher rates of poverty than younger and married women. More than 80 percent of women 65 and over live alone. Almost half of all these women have incomes below $5,000, compared with fewer than one man in five.

Official government family budget estimates were last issued in 1981. For a family of four living in metropolitan areas they showed a low level of $15,323, an intermediate level of $25,893, and a high level of $39,117. For a retired couple the corresponding figures were $7,226, $10,226, and $15,078.

Average real family income fell by 5.3 percent among blacks between 1980 and 1983, the largest decline of any group. In 1984, 29 percent of families had one earner, 15 percent had no earner, 56 percent two or more earners. In 1981, earned income for families with more than one earner was $31,919, compared with $21,320 for one-earner families. Where husband and wife worked full time the average was $34,789.

In the 1965–1969 period, inflation averaged 3.4 percent and unemployment 3.8 percent. For 1981–1985 the inflation average was 7.8 percent and the unemployment average 8.3 percent. These facts and those shown in the graphs and tables deal with the economic trends and forces that are central to human and social outcomes. We think they are useful for those concerned with poverty and who need to have information, however abbreviated, on the dimensions of wealth and affluence. Attention to economic issues underscores the degree to which all of us may be vulnerable to economic change and misfortune regardless of how hard we work to provide for ourselves and our families. From this perspective, more responsive and effective social and economic protections may well emerge.

TABLE 2.1. GROSS NATIONAL PRODUCT (GNP) IN CURRENT AND CONSTANT (1982) DOLLARS, 1978–1985

Real rates of growth were lower than nominal rates and on occasion were negative. Real growth in the first five Reagan years averaged 2.3 percent per year.

	Current Dollars		Constant Dollars	
Year	GNP (in billions)	Annual Percentage Change	GNP (in billions)	Annual Percentage Change
1978	$2,249.7	—	$3,115.2	—
1979	2,508.2	11.5	3,192.4	2.5
1980	2,732.0	8.9	3,187.1	−0.2
1981	3,052.6	11.7	3,248.8	1.9
1982	3,166.0	3.7	3,166.0	−2.5
1983	3,401.6	7.4	3,277.7	3.5
1984	3,774.7	11.0	3,492.0	6.5
1985	3,988.5	5.7	3,570.0	2.2

Source: U.S. Congress, Joint Economic Committee, *Economic Indicators* (Washington, D.C.: U.S. Government Printing Office, April 1986), pp. 1–3.

FIGURE 2.1. PER CAPITA GROSS NATIONAL PRODUCT (GNP), 1970–1984

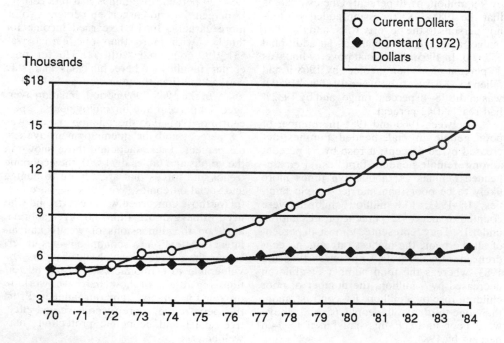

Source: Data from *Statistical Abstract of the United States, 1986*, p. 433.

TABLE 2.2 U.S. BALANCE OF PAYMENTS, 1960–1985 (IN MILLIONS)

The United States earned an export surplus every year from 1894 through 1970. By 1985 import surpluses were at record levels. Declines in petroleum imports were more then offset by increased imports of automobiles and other consumer products and capital goods.

Year	Merchandise			Balance, All Goods and Services[a]	Balance On Current Account[b]
	Exports	Imports	Net Balance		
1960	$19,650	$14,758	$4,892	$5,132	$2,824
1965	26,461	21,510	4,951	8,285	5,432
1970	42,469	39,866	2,603	5,625	2,331
1975	107,088	98,185	8,903	22,729	18,116
1980	224,269	249,749	−25,480	8,950	1,873
1981	237,085	265,063	−27,978	13,186	6,339
1982	211,198	247,642	−36,444	84	−8,051
1983	201,712	268,928	−67,216	−37,141	−45,994
1984	219,916	334,023	−114,107	−95,945	−107,358
1985	213,990	338,279	−124,289	−102,880	−117,664

[a]Military and travel, transportation, and other services
[b]Includes remittances, pensions.
Sources: *Economic Report of the President, 1986*, pp. 366, 373; and *Economic Indicators* (April 1986), p. 36.

TABLE 2.3. U.S. PRIVATE INVESTMENTS ABROAD AND FOREIGN INVESTMENTS IN THE UNITED STATES, 1977 AND 1984

U.S. assets in other countries continued to increase in this period; investments in the United States by other countries grew much faster, led by direct investment in U.S. land, business, real estate, and other assets.

Category	1977 (in billions)	1984 (in billions)	Percentage Increase
U.S. assets abroad			
Total	$195.4	$323.3	65.5
Direct investment	146.0	233.4	59.9
Foreign securities	49.4	89.9	82.0
Foreign assets in the U.S.			
Total	209.1	502.3	140.2
Direct investment	34.6	159.6	361.3
Corporate securities	51.2	128.2	150.4
U.S. government securities	123.3	214.5	74.0

Source: *Economic Report of the President, 1986*, p. 371.

TABLE 2.4. MONEY INCOME OF FAMILIES AND UNRELATED INDIVIDUALS, 1950–1984 (PERCENTAGE)

Income shares remain highly skewed. In 1983 the poorest 40 percent of families received the lowest share of total income and the richest 40 percent the highest share since the data were first gathered by the U.S. Bureau of the Census in 1947.

Income Group (Upper Limit)	1950	1960	1970	1975	1979	1983	1984
Lowest fifth	4.5	4.8	5.4	5.4	5.3	4.7	4.7
Second fifth	12.0	12.2	12.2	11.8	11.6	11.1	11.0
Third fifth	17.4	17.8	17.6	17.6	17.5	17.1	17.0
Fourth fifth	23.2	23.7	23.6	23.9	24.1	24.4	24.4
Highest fifth	42.2	40.7	40.5	40.7	41.6	42.7	42.9
Top 5 percent	17.2	15.7	15.5	15.4	15.7	15.8	16.0

Sources: U.S. Bureau of the Census, *Current Population Reports* (Washington, D.C.: U.S. Government Printing Office, Series P-60, Nos. 118, 140 [1982], 134 [1981], 129 [1980]); and *Statistical Abstract of the United States, 1979*, p. 452; *1981*, p. 438; *1982–83*, p. 435; *1985*, p. 448; and *1986*, p. 452.

TABLE 2.5. MEDIAN INCOME OF FAMILIES BY FAMILY TYPE AND RACE, WITH HOUSEHOLDER WORKING YEAR ROUND, FULL TIME, 1983 AND 1984

Major differences are related to race and ethnicity, marital status, and number of earners. Female householders received the lowest incomes in all groups shown.

Category	Number (in thousands)	1983	1984	Percentage Change (1984 dollars)
All families	62,706	$24,549	$26,433	3.3[b]
White families	54,400	25,719	27,686	3.3[b]
Married couple families	45,643	27,660	30,058	4.2[b]
Wife in paid labor force	23,979	32,549	35,176	3.7[b]
Wife not in paid labor force	21,664	22,333	24,246	4.1[b]
Male householder, no wife present	1,816	23,125	25,110	4.2[b]
Female householder, no husband present	6,941	13,713	15,134	5.9[b]
Black families	6,778	14,532	15,432	1.9
Married couple families	3,469	21,858	23,418	2.8
Wife in paid labor force	2,221	26,416	28,775	4.5
Wife not in paid labor force	1,248	13,849	14,502	0.4
Male householder, no wife present	344	15,474	15,724	−2.5
Female householder, no husband present	2,964	8,028	8,648	3.3[b]
Householder of Hispanic origin[a]	3,939	16,907	18,833	6.8[b]
Married couple families	2,824	20,103	22,599	7.8[b]
Wife in paid labor force	1,387	24,404	27,609	8.5
Wife not in paid labor force	1,437	15,967	17,160	3.0
Male householder, no wife present	210	18,130	18,578	−1.7
Female householder, no husband present	905	7,876	8,452	2.9

[a]May be of any race.
[b]Indicates statistically significant change at the 95 percent confidence level.
Source: *Money, Income and Poverty Status of Families and Persons in the United States, 1984*, pp. 6–8.

TABLE 2.6. MEDIAN FAMILY INCOME (1983 DOLLARS), 1969–1983, WITH PERCENTAGE OF CHANGE

Income of all families measured in constant dollars rose in the 1969–1979 period and declined in the 1979–1983 period. Female householders experienced the smallest increase in the earlier years and the largest decline thereafter; their average income in 1983 was 47.9 percent of the income of all families.

Year	All Families	Married-Couple Families	Female Householder, No Husband Present
1969	$25,636	$27,179	$13,105
1970	25,317	26,982	13,068
1971	25,301	27,036	12,580
1972	26,473	28,347	12,721
1973	27,017	29,208	12,996
1974	26,066	28,129	13,108
1975	25,395	27,521	12,669
1976	26,179	28,358	12,621
1977	26,320	28,963	12,766
1978	26,938	29,534	13,037
1979	26,885	29,413	13,562
1980	25,418	27,979	12,585
1981	24,525	27,457	12,006
1982	24,187	26,856	11,853
1983	24,549	27,268	11,769
Percentage of Change			
1969–1979	+4.9	+8.2	+3.5
1979–1983	−8.6	−9.3	−13.1

Source: U.S. Bureau of the Census, "Population Profiles of the United States, 1983–84," in Current Population Reports (Series P-23, No 145, Washington, D.C.: U.S. Government Printing Office, 1985), pp. 42–43; and "Money, Income and Poverty Status of Families and Persons in the United States, 1984," in *Current Population Reports* (Series P-60, No. 149, 1985), p. 2.

FIGURE 2.2 MEDIAN FAMILY INCOME, 1970–1984

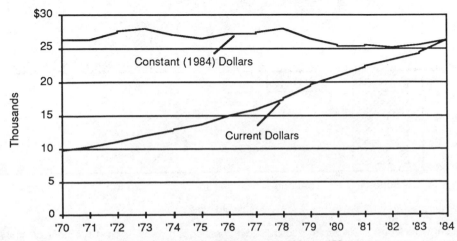

Source: Data from *Statistical Abstract of the United States, 1986*, p. 450.

TABLE 2.7. MEDIAN FAMILY INCOME BY NUMBER OF EARNERS AND RACE OF HOUSEHOLDER, 1983

Differences in income reflect race and the number of earners. The black-white difference is smallest in two-earner families.

Number of Earners	Median Family Income			Black-White Median Family Income Ratio	
	All Races[a]	White	Black	All Families	Families With Worker[b]
All families	$24,666	$25,838	$14,435	.56	.74
No earners	10,438	11,883	5,183	.44	—
1 earner	19,409	20,710	11,779	.57	.63
2 earners	29,808	30,357	24,396	.80	.84
3 earners	37,327	38,025	29,226	.77	.80
4 or more earners	47,732	48,540	36,727	.76	.85

[a]Includes races not shown.
[b]With full-time, year-round workers as householders.
Source: *Statistical Abstract of the United States, 1986*, p. 453.

FIGURE 2.3. CHANGE IN FAMILIES' REAL DISPOSABLE INCOME, 1980–1984 (PERCENTAGE)

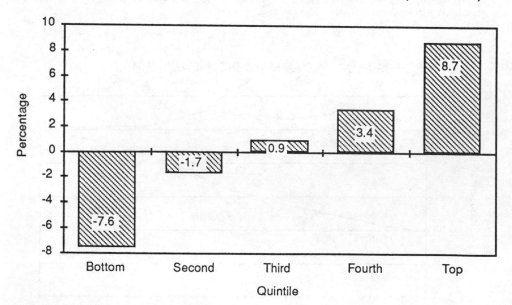

Source: Data from J. Palmer & I. Sawhill, Eds., *The Reagan Record: An Assessment of America's Changing Domestic Priorities* (Cambridge, Mass.: Ballinger Publishing Co., 1984), p. 321.

TABLE 2.8. SELECTED CHARACTERISTICS OF HOUSEHOLDS BY MEAN MONTHLY HOUSEHOLD CASH INCOME AND MEANS-TESTED PROGRAM PARTICIPATION STATUS; MONTHLY AVERAGE, OCTOBER–DECEMBER 1984

Important differences are related to geography, race and ethnic origin, age, and type of household. Benefits are very important to blacks, the disabled, female heads of household, and people over 65; they are significant to several other population groups.

Characteristics	Total (in thousands)	Mean Monthly Household Cash Income Value	One or More Members Receiving Means-Tested: Cash Benefits Percentage of Total	Food Stamps Percentage of Total
All households[a]	84,945	$2,327	8.4	7.2
Race and Hispanic origin of householder:				
White	73,620	2,429	6.5	5.1
Black	9,467	1,470	23.0	22.7
Hispanic origin[b]	4,105	1,753	17.7	15.7
Region:				
Northeast[c]	18,432	2,414	8.6	7.1
Midwest	21,463	2,261	8.2	7.0
South	28,786	2,192	8.7	8.7
West	16,265	2,555	8.0	4.8
Type of household:				
Family households	61,237	2,668	8.4	7.6
Married couple families	9,235	2,920	4.4	3.4
Female householder, no husband present with own children under 18 years	6,084	1,205	34.3	38.5
All other family households	5,918	2,078	15.4	10.2
Nonfamily households				
Male households	10,101	1,809	6.3	4.0
Female households	13,607	1,177	10.1	7.9
Age of householder:				
15 to 24 years	5,631	1,448	9.5	11.1
25 to 34 years	19,872	2,169	7.3	8.8
35 to 44 years	17,158	2,833	6.2	6.6
45 to 54 years	12,273	3,010	8.2	6.0
55 to 64 years	12,468	2,686	8.8	5.6
65 years and over	17,543	1,560	11.4	6.7
Work disability status of householder:				
Householder 16 to 64 years	67,399	2,527	7.7	7.3
With work disability	9,339	1,739	22.8	18.3
With retirement disability income	4,301	1,566	28.5	16.9
With no work disability	58,060	2,653	5.2	5.5

[a]Excludes persons in farm households and group quarters.
[b]Persons of Hispanic origin may be of any race.
[c]Formerly the North Central Region.
Source: U.S. Bureau of the Census, "Economic Characteristics of Households," in *Current Population Reports* (Series P-70, No. 6, Washington, D.C.: U.S. Government Printing Office, 1984), p. 24.

FIGURE 2.4. POVERTY AMONG CHILDREN IN THE UNITED STATES, 1959–1984

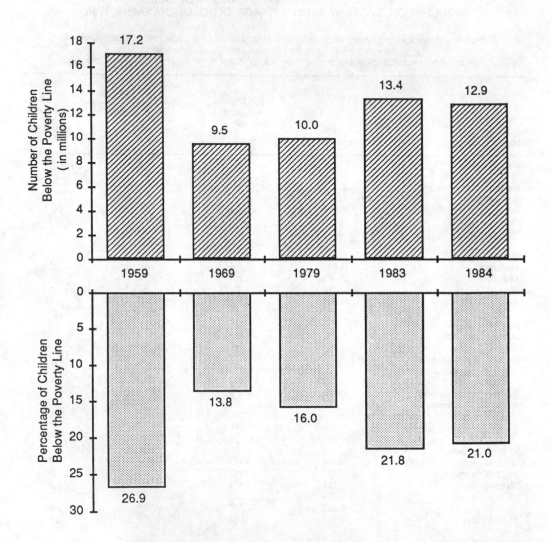

Source: *Statistical Abstract of the United States, 1986,* p. 458.

TABLE 2.9. PART-TIME WORK AND POVERTY STATUS OF PERSONS AGED 22–64, 1980 AND 1983

The proportion of poor people who work grew during this period. Part-time work shields only partially from poverty; unemployment directly affects poverty status; women in all categories are more vulnerable to poverty than men.

Category		Percentage Poor		
		Total	Men	Women
Total	1980	11	6	24
	1983	15	10	27
Worked part year or part time	1980	18	14	27
	1983	24	18	35
Worked full time	1980	2	2	3
	1983	4	3	4
Worked at all	1980	6	5	13
	1983	9	9	16
Did not work at all	1980	46	30	60
	1983	50	36	64

Sources: *Social Security Bulletin, Annual Statistical Supplement, 1980*, p. 63; and *Social Security Bulletin, Annual Statistical Supplement, 1984–85*, p. 74.

TABLE 2.10. POVERTY STATUS OF PERSONS 65 AND OLDER, 1983

Women in poverty over 65 outnumber men. Older individuals living alone are disproportionately poor, both men and women.

Category	Total (in thousands)	Percentage Poor
Total number of people	26,291	14.1
Unrelated individuals	8,591	26.5
Living in families	15,977	8.9
Male—Total	10,748	10.0
Unrelated individuals	1,865	22.1
Living in families	8,878	7.4
Female—Total	15,542	17.0
Unrelated individuals	6,727	27.7
Living in families	8,799	8.8

Source: *Social Security Bulletin, Annual Statistical Supplement, 1984–85*, p. 73.

FIGURE 2.5. POVERTY IN THE UNITED STATES, 1965–1984

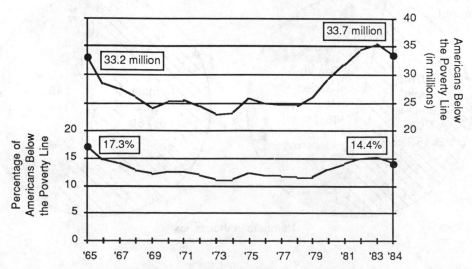

Sources: Center on Budget and Policy Priorities, *Smaller Slices of the Pie* (Washington, D.C.: Author, 1986); and data from *Statistical Abstract of the United States, 1986*, pp. 450, 457.

FIGURE 2.6. POVERTY IN THE UNITED STATES,
BY RACE, AGE, TYPE OF HOUSEHOLD, AND SEX, 1984

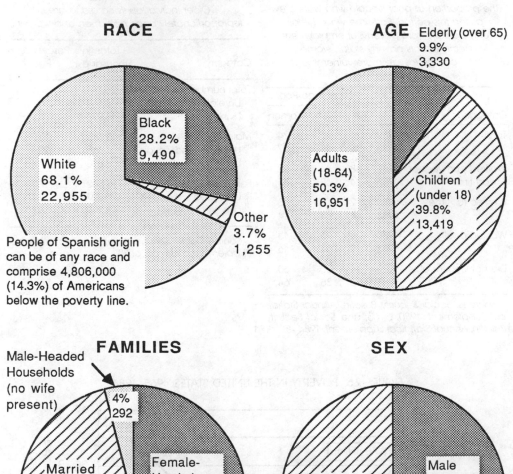

RACE

White
68.1%
22,955

Black
28.2%
9,490

Other
3.7%
1,255

People of Spanish origin
can be of any race and
comprise 4,806,000
(14.3%) of Americans
below the poverty line.

AGE

Elderly (over 65)
9.9%
3,330

Adults
(18-64)
50.3%
16,951

Children
(under 18)
39.8%
13,419

FAMILIES

Male-Headed
Households
(no wife
present)

4%
292

Married
Couple
Families
47.9%
3,488

Female-
Headed
Households
48.1%
3,498

SEX

Female
56.9%
19,163

Male
43.1%
14,537

Numbers in thousands

Source: Data from *Smaller Slices of the Pie,* p. 9.

SECTION 3. EMPLOYMENT, UNEMPLOYMENT, AND UNDEREMPLOYMENT

The lives of most people depend on employment and the income and benefits it provides. The most marked change in the American labor force and labor market has been the large-scale participation of women. In 1954, white men were 62.5 percent of the labor force; in 1970, 55.6 percent; in 1983—for the first time—less than 50 percent.

The second major change has been the stagnation of earnings and decline of job quality—measured by income, stability, and opportunity—accompanied by the long-term increase in unemployment and underemployment among all groups. One recent study[1] predicts that employment in low-paying industries will grow more rapidly in the future and that in high-paying industries, more slowly. By 1978 the service share of U.S. jobs—51 percent—was higher than in any other major industrial country. Other economists note that jobs linked to exports, which pay relatively well, have declined and low-paying jobs have increased in recent years. Total jobs increased in the United States by almost 13 million between 1973 and 1979; from 1980 to 1985, the total job increase was 7 million.

Between 1973 and 1984 employment in the United States grew by 16.7 million in expanding sectors and declined by 2.1 million in shrinking sectors. Major sources of growth included health care (2.4 million), eating and drinking places (2.3 million), business services (2.1 million), and state and local government (1.1 million). Losers included primary metals (412,000), textile mills (260,000), apparel (256,000), fabricated metals (185,000), and retail sales (163,000).

At the same time, measured unemployment remained at or above 7 percent from 1980 on, well above the average for the postwar period prior to 1980. In 1979, the total of discouraged workers and workers working part time for economic reasons was two-thirds of the number counted as unemployed; by 1984 these two groups were four-fifths of the (higher) number of unemployed persons; while the unemployment percentage rose by 39 percent, the number of part-time workers rose by 70 percent and the number of discouraged workers by 66 percent. In 1985, about 5.5 million part-time workers wanted full-time work. The number of self-employed reached a low of 5.2 million in 1970 (reflecting the decline in agriculture), then increased to 9.1 million in 1983; almost half are 45 or older, seven in ten are male, and most are white. The increase in part-time and temporary employment further reduces coverage for health insurance, disability and workers' compensation, and other protections and benefits.

The weekly earnings of employed workers, measured in constant (1977) dollars, rose from $168.05 in September 1981 to $172.40 in June 1985—an increase of 2.6 percent. The index of hourly earnings, with 1977 equal to 100, stood at 92.1 in 1981 and 94.2 in 1985. In 1983, when the median family income was $24,580, almost 40 percent of families earning between $15,000 and $25,000, more than half of all families earning between $25,000 and $59,000, and over 60 percent of families earning more than $50,000 were families with two or more earners. Overall earnings of two-earner families were 20 percent higher than the average for all families and 54 percent higher than earnings of single-earner families.

A federal study estimated that between 1979 and 1984, 11.5 million people lost jobs as a result of plant closings or relocations. Sixty percent found new jobs; of this group 45 percent took pay cuts and two-thirds were earning less than two-thirds of their previous earnings. Of the 11.5 million, 5.1 million had held their previous jobs for three years or more. Of workers displaced after three years or more, 43 percent were out of work for at least 27 weeks and nearly one-fourth for a year or longer. In manufacturing, where most of the job losses occurred, average hourly earnings were $9.18 in 1984; in service employment the average was $7.52. At a symposium marking the fortieth anniversary of the Employment Act of 1946, the chairman of the Joint Economic Committee of Congress observed that young men who left home in the 1950s and 1960s could expect, by age 30,

---

[1] B. Bluestone & B. Harrison. (1984). *Storm Clouds on the Horizon: Labor Market Crisis and Industrial Policy*. Brookline, Mass.: Economic Education Project.

to be earning one-third more than their fathers had earned when *they* left home. In 1985, on the other hand, 30-year-old men were earning 10 percent less than their fathers had under similar circumstances.

Education and occupational status are highly correlated. About two-thirds of men and three-fifths of women with college degrees hold managerial or professional jobs; 80 percent of men and 78 percent of women in these jobs had some college education. At the other end of the spectrum, labor force participation drops off for those with less than a high school education. For those with some high school or more education, the participation rate for women is less than for men, with the smallest difference for those with four years or more of college. At each level of school completed, men are likely to earn more than women; the difference narrows as the level of education increases.

While black labor force participation overall is below white, participation rates of blacks exceeded those of whites at each level of education except the lowest; many more blacks than whites enter the labor force at lower educational levels. The median income of blacks was 57 percent that of whites in 1960, 56 percent in 1981. Educational improvements for blacks were offset by lower earnings at the same educational level, higher rates of unemployment and underemployment, and a much larger share of female-headed single-parent families. In families with two working parents, the average income of black families rose from 73 percent that of whites in 1978 to 84 percent in 1981. Between 1981 and 1985, long-term unemployment among blacks rose by 72 percent. Hispanic workers' earnings exceed those of blacks in all major sectors except trade and manufacturing.

Most working women hold full-time jobs; among married and divorced women, whether or not they had children younger than 18, the proportion holding full-time jobs approached or exceeded 80 percent by 1984. Sixteen percent of working women earned more than their husbands in 1983. Most of these had college degrees; the majority were aged 25 to 44. Earnings of women working full time averaged 64 percent of men's earnings in white-collar jobs and 72 percent in blue-collar jobs in 1983. In 1980, 48 percent of working women were in occupations that were predominantly (80 percent or more) female; 72 percent of men worked in male-dominated occupations. Four sectors—services, trade, government, and manufacturing—employed 83.5 percent of working women and 71.4 percent of working men. Seven of the 10 occupations providing the largest number of new jobs for women between 1970 and 1980 were predominantly female. Women increased their share of jobs between 1970 and 1980 among managers, sales supervisors, production supervisors, and janitors and cleaners. The share of women in some female-dominated occupations—secretaries, nurses, bookkeepers, cashiers, nurses, and clerks—increased over this period; in a few—elementary school teachers and waiters and waitresses—the female share decreased. In some traditionally male occupations—including bartenders, bakers, bus drivers, bank officials, pharmacists, and scientists—the share of jobs held by women increased in the early 1980s.

Calculations by the Children's Defense Fund show that more women than men and more blacks than whites earned less than $300 per week in 1984. Between 1970 and 1980, white-collar and service jobs grew by 18 percent in central cities and blue-collar jobs declined by 5 percent. In suburbs both categories grew—white-collar and service jobs by 53 percent and blue-collar jobs by 20 percent.

The official minimum wage was raised (and its coverage broadened) at irregular intervals until it reached its present level, $3.35 per hour, in 1980. Eleven percent of people working in 1984 earned less than that amount. Unemployment among white teenagers shows no discernible relationship to these increases and extensions. In the 1940s, black teenage unemployment was equal to or lower than that of whites; by 1985 it was more than double the white rate.

Average pay in 1983 varied among metropolitan areas from a high of $21,562 in the Houston-Galveston-Brazonia area to a low of $15,223 in the Providence-Pawtucket-Woonsocket area, a difference of $6,339. The median was $18,622 in the Hartford, Connecticut, area. High-paying areas included Detroit–Ann Arbor, San Francisco–Oakland–San Jose, and New York–Northern New

Jersey–Long Island–Southern Connecticut. Those on the low end included Miami–Fort Lauderdale, Buffalo–Niagara Falls, and Portland-Vancouver.

One important effect of large-scale immigration on the economies of large cities has been to depress wages and expand the size of the low-wage sectors in manufacturing and services. The effect is most marked in cities with large concentrations of Hispanics—Los Angeles, New York, Chicago, Miami, and San Antonio have the largest numbers.

The Office of Technology Assessment estimated that about 6,000 workers die of injuries each year, 25 per working day, and that on each working day there are at least 10,000 injuries that result in lost work time and 45,000 that require medical attention or result in restricted activity.

Data for metropolitan areas show that unionization declined in all areas among production workers. The highest unionized shares in 1984 were in transportation and utilities (85 percent), manufacturing (60 percent), and wholesale trade (42 percent). Wage increases negotiated under collective bargaining decreased through 1985, and many union members experienced wage and other concessions in collective bargaining after 1979.

A Joint Economic Committee study in 1984 estimated that an increase in unemployment comparable to the one that occurred between 1973 and 1974 would increase total mortality in the United States by 45,936, of which 28,510 would be cardiovascular deaths, and would cause increases—some very large—in such social indicators as arrests, suicides, assaults, and mental hospital admissions.

The picture presented here reflects the degree to which economic security based on gainful employment has been eroded for many as a result of major shifts in the structure and operation of labor markets and in the economy and as a result of limited private and public ability to facilitate the needed adjustments and responses. Although larger economic factors affect the ability of the economy to employ and provide for all those who need and seek work, energetic and imaginative labor market policies and programs could do much to improve our systems of education, training, and employment.

TABLE 3.1. CIVILIAN LABOR FORCE PARTICIPATION BY SEX AND RACE, 1970–1984

Participation rates for men of all races declined, and female participation increased dramatically. The decline among men applied to all age groups. Female participation rates rose for all age groups except those 65 and older.

	Labor Force (in thousands)			Participation Rate (percentage)		
	1970	1980	1984	1970	1980	1984
Total, age 16 and over	82,771	106,544	113,544	60.4	63.8	64.4
Men	51,288	61,453	63,835	79.7	77.4	76.4
Women	31,543	45,487	49,709	43.3	51.5	53.6
White						
Men	46,035	54,473	56,062	80.0	78.2	77.1
Women	27,521	39,127	42,431	42.6	51.2	53.3
Black and other						
Men	5,194	6,980	6,126	76.5	71.5	70.8
Women	4,024	6,359	5,907	49.5	53.6	55.2

Sources: U.S. Bureau of Labor Statistics, *Monthly Labor Review* (Washington, D.C.: U.S. Government Printing Office, November 1983), p. 5; for 1984: *Statistical Abstract of the United States, 1986*, pp. 392, 394.

TABLE 3.2. MALES AND FEMALES IN THE LABOR FORCE, 1950–1985

The number of women in the labor force increased faster than men in absolute and relative terms throughout this 35-year period. In 1985 women were 44 percent of the labor force.

	Male	Female
Year	Number in Civilian Labor Force (in thousands)	Number in Civilian Labor Force (in thousands)
1950	41,578	18,389
1960	43,904	21,874
1970	48,990	31,543
1975	51,857	37,475
1980	57,186	45,487
1985	64,412	51,050

Source: *Economic Report of the President, 1986*, pp. 290, 293.

TABLE 3.3. OCCUPATIONAL GROUPS WITH 25 PERCENT OR MORE FEMALE REPRESENTATION, 1983

Women's earnings, regardless of occupational group or size of female representation, are substantially lower than men's.

Occupational Group	Total Employent (in thousands)	Percentage Female	Female-to-Male Earnings (percentage)
Executive, administrative, managerial	17,451	40.9	69.6
Professional specialty occupations[a]	9,334	46.8	71.9
Writers, artists, entertainers	831	38.5	72.0
Technical, sales, and administrative support	21,641	62.5	62.8
Sales	6,313	39.0	51.0
Administrative and clerical	12,755	77.7	68.8
Service (household, child care, protective)	7,321	49.1	67.5
Other service	5,590	57.1	81.0
Operators, fabricators, and laborers	13,319	26.2	66.8

[a]Includes 358,000 social workers; other groups include: engineers, architects, scientists, nurses, teachers, librarians, and lawyers.

Source: *Monthly Labor Review* (January 1985), pp. 55–59.

TABLE 3.4. MOTHERS IN THE LABOR FORCE, BY RACE AND AGE OF YOUNGEST CHILD, 1985

Women's participation increased with the age of the youngest child.
White mothers who maintain families are somewhat more likely to be working or looking for work than similar black women who maintain familes, but black married women are more likely to be in the labor force than are whites.

Category of Youngest Child	Married Women, Husbands Present		Women Who Maintain Families	
	(in thousands)	Participation Rate	(in thousands)	Participation Rate
No children under 18	12,620	48.2	2,117	50.7
White	11,452	47.5	1,592	51.9
Black	928	56.1	479	46.6
1 year or under	2,562	49.4	277	38.0
White	2,260	48.6	167	39.2
Black	216	63.7	109	38.4
2 years	1,145	54.0	233	55.7
White	999	52.7	152	55.9
Black	107	69.9	75	54.0
3 to 5 years	2,591	58.6	761	61.2
White	2,186	56.6	490	64.6
Black	295	73.8	260	56.0
6 to 13 years	5,713	68.1	1,975	75.7
White	5,034	67.7	1,371	78.1
Black	477	73.5	556	70.9
14 to 17 years	2,756	67.0	1,056	78.5
White	2,471	66.3	802	82.1
Black	215	74.1	227	68.4
All mothers with children under 18	14,766	61.0	4,302	67.8

Source: *Monthly Labor Review* (February 1986), p. 44.

TABLE 3.5. OCCUPATIONAL DISTRIBUTION OF EMPLOYED PERSONS, 1961–1983
(PERCENTAGES)

*This period showed a growing white-collar and service economy, with women and blacks
securing increasing shares of the better jobs and whites and males
representing significant shares of professional, technical, managerial, and craft jobs. Black
males had a higher share than whites in declining job categories.*

Category	1961	1971	1981	1983
White-collar workers—total	43.9	48.3	52.7	55.4
Professional, technical, managerial	22.5	25.0	27.9	27.4
Sales and clerical	21.4	23.4	24.9	28.0
White-collar workers—males	38.1	40.9	42.9	44.0
Professional, technical, managerial	25.0	28.3	30.5	27.3
Sales and clerical	12.9	12.6	12.4	16.7
White-collar workers—females	55.6	60.5	65.9	67.7
Professional, technical, managerial	17.5	19.0	24.4	25.2
Sales and clerical	38.1	41.5	41.5	42.5
White-collar workers—whites	47.1	50.6	54.3	56.0
Professional, technical, managerial	24.3	26.4	29.0	27.3
Sales and clerical	22.8	24.3	25.3	28.7
White-collar workers—blacks and others	16.1	29.1	41.1	39.5[a]
Professional, technical, managerial	7.4	13.1	19.7	16.8
Sales and clerical	8.8	16.0	21.4	22.7
Blue-collar workers—total	36.0	34.4	31.1	28.2
Craft and kindred	13.1	12.9	12.6	12.2
Operatives and laborers	22.9	21.5	18.6	16.0
Blue-collar workers—males	46.0	45.9	44.3	40.7
Craft and kindred	19.2	19.9	20.7	19.9
Operatives and laborers	26.7	26.0	23.7	20.8
Blue-collar workers—females	16.4	15.4	13.6	12.0
Craft and kindred	1.0	1.3	1.9	2.3
Operatives and laborers	15.3	14.1	11.7	9.7
Blue-collar workers—whites	35.6	33.7	30.7	27.7
Craft and kindred	13.9	13.5	13.1	12.6
Operatives and laborers	21.7	20.3	17.6	15.1
Blue-collar workers—blacks and others	39.4	39.9	34.8	33.1[a]
Craft and kindred	6.2	7.9	9.2	9.0
Operatives and laborers	33.2	32.0	25.7	24.1

(Continued on next page)

TABLE 3.5. (continued)

Category	1961	1971	1981	1983
Service workers—total	12.6	13.5	13.4	13.7
Private household	3.1	1.9	1.0	1.0
Other	9.5	11.6	12.3	12.8
Service workers—males	6.7	8.2	8.9	9.7
Private household	0.1	0.1	0.1	0.1
Other	6.6	8.1	8.8	9.7
Service workers—females	24.2	22.2	19.4	18.9
Private household	9.0	4.9	2.3	2.1
Other	15.2	17.4	17.1	16.8
Service workers—whites	10.2	11.8	12.2	12.5
Private household	1.8	1.2	0.8	0.8
Other	8.4	10.6	11.4	11.7
Service workers—blacks and others	31.7	27.6	22.4	24.5[a]
Private household	14.2	7.3	2.9	2.9
Other	17.5	20.3	19.6	21.5
Service workers—Hispanics[b]				17.7
Private household	—	—	—	1.6
Other	—	—	—	16.1
Farm workers—total	7.5	3.8	2.7	3.7[c]
Male	9.3	5.1	3.9	5.5
Female	3.9	1.7	1.1	1.3
Whites	—	—	—	3.8
Blacks and others	—	—	1.5	3.0[a]
Hispanics	—	—	—	5.8

[a]Black only.
[b]1983 only.
[c]Farming, forestry, fishing.
Sources: U. S. Department of Labor, *Employment and Training Report of the President, 1982* (Washington, D.C.: U.S. Government Printing Office, 1982), pp. 178–180; and *Handbook of Labor Statistics, 1985*, p. 48; for Hispanics: National Commission for Employment Policy, *Hispanics and Jobs: Barrier to Progress* (Report No. 14; Washington, D.C.: U.S. Government Printing Office, September 1984), p.22.

TABLE 3.6. YEARS OF SCHOOL COMPLETED BY CIVILIAN LABOR FORCE, BY RACE AND ETHNIC ORIGIN, 1962 AND 1984

Racial differences in education narrowed over this period; Hispanics have the lowest levels of education.

| | Percentage of Group | | | | | | | |
| | All | | White | | Black | | Hispanic Origin | |
Education	1962	1984	1962	1984	1962	1984	1962	1984
College								
4 years or more	11.0	20.9	11.8	21.6	4.8	11.6	5.7	8.3
1–3 years	10.7	19.0	11.3	19.1	5.7	18.5	10.6	15.1
High school								
4 years	32.1	40.7	33.5	40.9	21.0	41.5	28.4	31.2
1–3 years	19.3	13.0	18.8	12.4	23.2	18.4	20.6	18.2
Elementary school								
5–8 years	22.4	5.5	21.4	5.2	29.8	8.3	23.0	19.2
Less than 5 years	4.6	1.0	3.3	0.8	15.4	1.7	11.8	7.4

Source: *Handbook of Labor Statistics 1985,* pp. 164–165, 167–168.

TABLE 3.7. LABOR FORCE, EMPLOYMENT, UNEMPLOYMENT, ANNUAL AVERAGES, 1948–1985[a]

Unemployment rates were relatively low until 1970 and substantially higher thereafter. The labor force grew faster than the number of jobs.

Year	Civilian Labor Force	Employed	Unemployed	Unemployment (Percentage)
1948	60,621	58,343	2,276	3.8
1950	62,208	58,918	3,288	5.3
1955	65,023	62,170	2,852	4.4
1960	69,628	65,778	3,852	5.5
1965	74,455	71,088	3,355	4.5
1970	82,771	78,678	4,093	4.9
1975	93,775	85,846	7,929	8.5
1980	106,940	99,303	7,637	7.1
1981	108,670	100,397	8,273	7.6
1982	110,204	99,526	10,678	9.7
1983	111,550	100,834	10,717	9.6
1984	113,544	105,005	8,539	7.5
1985	115,461	107,150	8,312	7.2

[a]Numbers in thousands.

Source: U.S. Department of Labor, *Economic Report of the President, 1986* (Washington, D.C.: U.S. Government Printing Office, 1986), p. 288.

TABLE 3.8. ANNUAL UNEMPLOYMENT RATES BY SEX, RACE, AND ETHNIC CATEGORY, 1947–1985

Rates for all males and all females were close in the 1984–1985 period and moved in the same direction over the period shown. Rates by race, among both men and women, became sharply differentiated. Rates for Hispanics fell between the two, closer to black than to white rate.

Year	Total	Males				Females			
		All	White	Black and Other	Hispanic Origin	All	White	Black and Other	Hispanic Origin
1947	3.9	4.0	—	—	—	3.7	—	—	—
1952	3.0	2.8	2.5	5.2	—	3.6	3.3	5.7	—
1957	4.3	4.1	3.6	8.3	—	4.7	4.3	7.3	—
1962	5.5	5.2	4.6	10.9	—	6.2	5.5	11.0	—
1967	3.8	3.1	2.7	6.0	—	3.1	4.6	9.1	—
1972	5.6	5.0	4.5	8.9	—	6.6	5.9	11.4	—
1977	7.1	6.3	5.5	12.3	9.0	8.2	7.3	13.9	11.9
1978	6.1	5.3	4.6	11.0	7.7	7.2	6.2	13.0	11.3
1979	5.8	5.1	4.5	10.4	7.0	6.8	5.9	12.3	10.3
1980	7.1	6.9	6.1	13.2	9.7	7.4	6.5	13.1	10.7
1981	7.6	7.4	6.5	14.1	10.2	7.9	6.9	14.3	10.8
1982	9.7	8.8	7.8	17.8	12.0	8.3	7.3	15.4	12.6
1983	9.6	8.9	7.9	18.1	12.2	8.1	6.9	16.5	12.5
1984	7.5	7.4	6.4	16.4	10.5	7.6	6.5	15.4	11.1
1985	7.2	7.0	6.1	15.3	10.2	7.4	6.4	14.9	11.0

Sources: U.S. Bureau of Labor Statistics, *Handbook of Labor Statistics 1985*, pp. 71–73; *Employment in Perspective: Women in the Labor Force, Fourth Quarter 1985*, p. 85; and *Employment in Perspective: Minority Workers, Fourth Quarter 1985*, p. 2. (All Washington, D.C.: U.S. Government Printing Office, 1985.)

FIGURE 3.1. UNEMPLOYMENT RATE, 1978–1985 (PERCENTAGE)

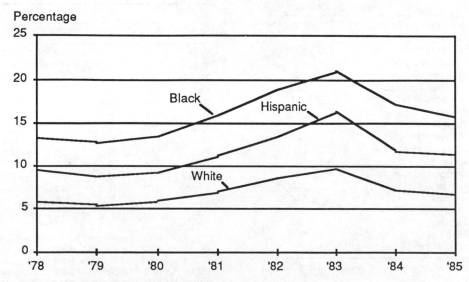

Source: *Statistical Abstract of the United States, 1986*, p. 407.

TABLE 3.9. SHORT-TERM AND LONG-TERM UNEMPLOYMENT, 1948–1985

Since 1972 fewer than half of the jobless have been unemployed for less than five weeks; many remain unemployed for 15 weeks or longer.

| Year | Percentage of All Unemployed | | | | Average Duration of Unemployment (weeks) |
	Less than 5 Weeks	5–14 Weeks	15–26 Weeks	27 Weeks and Over	
1948	57.1	29.3	8.5	5.1	—
1952	60.2	27.4	7.9	4.5	—
1957	49.3	31.1	11.2	8.4	—
1962	42.4	29.0	13.6	15.0	—
1967	54.9	30.1	9.1	5.9	—
1972	45.9	30.2	12.3	11.6	—
1977	41.7	30.4	13.1	14.8	—
1980	43.1	32.3	13.8	10.8	11.9
1981	41.7	30.7	13.6	14.0	13.7
1982	36.4	31.0	16.0	16.6	15.6
1983	33.3	27.4	15.4	23.9	20.0
1984	39.2	28.8	12.9	19.1	18.2
1985	42.1	30.2	12.3	15.4	15.6

Sources: *Handbook of Labor Statistics 1985,* p. 79; for 1984–1985 data: U.S. Bureau of Labor Statistics, *Employment and Earnings* (Washington, D.C.: U.S. Government Printing Office, January 1986), p. 202.

TABLE 3.10. UNEMPLOYMENT RATES, JULY 1985 (PERCENTAGE)

Teenagers, younger workers, and minorities in all categories are at greatest risk; government, white-collar, service, and mature workers are least vulnerable to unemployment.

Group	Percentage Unemployed
Black teenagers	41.3
White teenagers	16.3
All black persons	15.0
Young men aged 20–24	11.7
Persons of Hispanic origin	11.2
Young women aged 20–24	10.6
Women heads of households	10.2
Part-time workers	9.5
Full-time workers	7.0
All white persons	6.4
Men aged 20 and over	5.6
Married women	5.7
Women aged 20 and over	5.7
Married men	4.4
Farm workers	14.3
Government workers	4.1
Manufacturing workers	8.0
Construction	13.4
Finance and service industries	7.5

Source: *Monthly Labor Review* (January 1986), pp. 89, 90.

TABLE 3.11. YOUTH UNEMPLOYMENT RATES BY AGE, 1948–1986

Youth unemployment rose relative to adult rates in the 1960s; the relationship stabilized in the 1970s, nonwhite youth unemployment rose sharply after 1970.

| Year | All | | | Nonwhite |
	16–24	16–19	20–24	16–19
1948	7.3	9.2	6.2	—
1950	9.3	12.1	7.7	—
1955	8.7	11.0	7.0	15.8
1960	11.2	14.7	8.7	24.4
1965	10.1	14.8	6.7	26.2
1970	11.0	15.3	8.2	19.1
1975	16.1	19.9	13.6	36.7
1980	13.8	17.8	11.5	35.4
1981	14.9	19.6	12.3	37.8
1982	17.8	23.2	14.9	43.9[b]
1983	—	22.4	14.5	48.5[b]
1986[a]	13.0	18.4	10.4	41.9

[a] January only.
[b] Black only.
Sources: *Employment and Training Report of the President, 1982,* pp. 159, 161; *Handbook of Labor Statistics 1985,* pp. 69, 72; for 1986: U.S. Bureau of Labor Statistics, *The Employment Situation* (Washington, D.C.: U.S. Government Printing Office, January 1986), Table A-9.

TABLE 3.12. DISPLACED WORKERS BY YEAR OF JOB LOSS, SEX, RACE, HISPANIC ORIGIN, AND EMPLOYMENT STATUS, JANUARY 1984[a]

Significant numbers of people who lost their jobs in these years remained without work one to four years later; blacks and Hispanics show this more than whites, but all are affected. Most continue to look for work, but some leave the labor force.

Category	Total[a] (in thousands)	Distribution by Employment Status in January 1984 (Percentage)[a]		
		Employed	Unemployed	Not in Labor Force
TOTAL				
Total, 20 years and over	5,091	60.1	25.5	14.4
Lost job in: 1979	567	63.2	14.1	22.7
1980	703	72.9	14.8	12.3
1981	1,016	66.8	16.6	16.7
1982	1,346	62.4	23.2	14.5
1983	1,447	45.7	43.6	10.6
Men				
Total, 20 years and over	3,328	63.6	27.1	9.2
Lost job in: 1979	344	68.3	15.5	16.2
1980	462	74.4	16.8	8.8
1981	670	71.5	18.2	10.3
1982	880	66.4	25.5	8.1
1983	965	48.5	44.2	7.3
Women				
Total, 20 years and over	1,763	53.4	22.5	24.2
Lost job in: 1979	223	55.3	11.9	32.8
1980	241	70.0	11.1	18.9
1981	346	57.5	13.5	29.0
1982	466	54.7	18.8	26.5
1983	482	40.1	42.6	17.3[b]
White				
Total, 20 years and over	4,397	62.6	23.4	13.9
Lost job in: 1979–1980	1,969	70.2	13.7	16.1
1982–1983	2,418	56.4	31.3	12.3
Black				
Total, 20 years and over	602	41.8	41.0	17.1
Lost job in: 1979–1981	278	50.0	28.7	21.3
1982–1983	324	34.8	51.7	13.6
Hispanic origin				
Total, 20 years and over	282	52.2	33.7	14.1
Lost job in: 1979–1981	99	62.7	12.9	24.3
1982–1983	180	47.0	44.4	8.5

[a]Data refer to persons with tenure of three or more years who lost or left a job between January 1979 and January 1984 because of plant closings or moves, slack work, or the abolishment of their positions or shifts; includes a small number of persons who did not report the year of job loss.

[b]Data for racial and Hispanic-origin groups will not sum to totals because data for "other races" group are not presented and Hispanics are included in both the white and black groups.

Source: U.S. Bureau of Labor Statistics, *Displaced Workers 1979–83* (Washington, D.C.: U.S. Government Printing Office, Bulletin 2240, 1984), p. 7.

TABLE 3.13. UNEMPLOYMENT RATES IN MAJOR METROPOLITAN AREAS, MAY, 1983–1985 (PERCENTAGE)

Unemployment rates vary widely; more cities were below than above the overall rate of unemployment.

City	1983	1984	1985	City	1983	1984	1985
Baltimore	7.5	6.2	5.3	Memphis	9.4	7.1	6.0
Boston	6.5	3.5	3.0	Milwaukee	10.1	6.4	5.7
Chicago	11.7	8.1	8.7	New Orleans	11.5	9.1	11.7
Cleveland	12.2	9.6	7.3	New York City	8.9	7.6	8.4
Columbus (Ohio)	9.7	8.1	5.5	Philadelphia	9.4	6.7	6.4
Dallas	5.7	3.4	4.4	San Antonio	6.3	4.6	5.4
Detroit	15.4	10.9	—	San Diego	9.0	5.9	5.0
Houston	10.1	6.4	7.3	San Francisco	8.4[a]	5.1	4.5
Indianapolis	8.7	6.9	6.0	Oakland		6.7	5.9
Jacksonville	8.2	5.5	4.0	San Jose	8.1	4.8	4.8
Los Angeles–Long Beach	10.2	7.1	7.0	Washington, D.C.	5.1	8.8	8.0

[a]In 1983, San Francisco–Oakland was classified as a single metropolitan area.

Sources: U.S. Bureau of Labor Statistics, *State and Metropolitan Area Employment and Unemployment, July 1983;* and *State and Metropolitan Area Employment and Unemployment, June 1985* (Washington, D.C.: U.S. Government Printing Office, 1983; 1985).

TABLE 3.14. MEDIAN WEEKLY EARNINGS OF DISPLACED WORKERS REEMPLOYED IN JANUARY 1984, BY INDUSTRY AND CLASS OF WORKER[a]

People reemployed in government and service jobs increased their earnings; for the rest the drop in earnings ranged from 16.4 percent for manufacturing workers to 7.3 percent for workers in wholesale and retail trade. The overall loss of earnings averaged 11.1 percent.

Industry and Class of Worker	Total (in thousands)	Median Weekly Earnings on Lost Job	Median Weekly Earnings on Job Held in January 1984	Percentage
Total, 20 years and over	3,058	$306	$272	88.9
Mining	91	429	325	75.8
Construction	220	334	309	92.5
Manufacturing	1,452	319	266	83.4
Transportation and public utilities	194	397	348	87.7
Wholesale and retail trade	450	275	255	92.7
Services	329	264	268	101.5
Government workers	157	262	270	103.1

[a]Data refer to persons with tenure of three or more years who lost or left a job between January 1979 and January 1984 because of plant closings or moves, slack work, or the abolishment of their positions or shifts; includes a small number of persons who did not report the year of job loss.

Source: *Displaced Workers 1979–83*, p. 28.

TABLE 3.15. FEMALE AND MALE WEEKLY EARNINGS BY OCCUPATION, 1983[a]

Sex differences were pervasive; women were most disadvantaged in banks and advertising agencies and were closest to males in health care, the postal service, teaching, law, and engineering.

Occupation	Weekly Earnings		Female as Percentage of Male
	Men	Women	
Health services			
Nursing aides and orderlies	$231	$186	80.5
Physicians	508	421	82.9
Health administrators	—	435	—
Educational services			
Editors and reporters	408	322	78.9
High school teachers	406	358	88.2
Elementary school teachers	404	351	86.9
College teachers	508	403	79.3
School administrators	577	401	69.5
Sales, marketing and financial services			
Cashiers	201	164	76.6
Real estate agents	458	307	67.0
Sales, retail and personal services	259	166	64.1
Insurance agents	423	295	69.7
Buyers	405	259	64.0
Advertising and marketing managers	614	367	59.8
Financial manager	573	359	62.7
Average weekly earnings, all occupations	379	252[b,c]	

Occupation	Weekly Earnings		Female as Percentage of Male
	Men	Women	
Professional and technical services			
Social workers	$398	$308	77.4
Social scientists	551	381	69.1
Computer programmers	503	406	80.7
Accountants	487	343	70.4
Lawyers	656	576	87.8
Engineers	602	486	80.7
Production workers			
Packers and wrappers	233	207	88.8
Stock clerks	308	246	79.9
Textile, apparel machine operators	229	170	—
Other service workers			
Postal clerks	441	407	92.3
Security guards	242	201	83.1
Bartenders	207	179	86.5
Janitors	236	188	79.7
Cooks	197	162	82.2
Waiters and waitresses	210	152	72.4
Bookkeepers	307	249	81.1
Secretaries, typists	340	250	73.5
Personnel specialists	513	339	66.1
Bus drivers	365	260	71.2

[a]Total employed, 70,976,000 (42,309,000 men, 28,667,000 women).
[b]Ratio female-to-male earnings, 66.5:100.
[c]Ratio female-to-male workers, 40.4:100.
Source: *Monthly Labor Review* (January 1985), pp. 55–59.

TABLE 3.16. WORKERS' SPENDABLE WEEKLY EARNINGS IN CONSTANT (1977)
DOLLARS, 1948–1981

Stagnation and decline of real earnings occurred in all sectors in the 1970s and continued through 1981 , often to levels at or below those of 15–20 years earlier.

Occupational Sector	1948	1958	1968	1973	1978	1981
Total	$122.19	$144.88	$165.99	$173.78	$167.95	$147.05
Mining	158.21	180.71	213.45	232.95	256.98	235.76
Construction	157.58	193.94	243.87	271.90	247.49	215.79
Manufacturing	131.69	157.04	189.98	195.77	199.69	178.24
Transportation, Public utilities	—	—	208.26	234.98	236.86	209.88
Wholesale & retail trades	101.74	122.60	137.57	137.87	132.04	114.10
Finance, insurance, real estate	113.43	136.58	157.94	156.58	149.71	133.69
Services	—	—	133.33	143.85	139.33	123.57

Source: *Employment and Training Report of the President, 1982,* pp. 227–230.

FIGURE 3.2 PRODUCTIVITY AND HOURLY COMPENSATION, 1970–1984

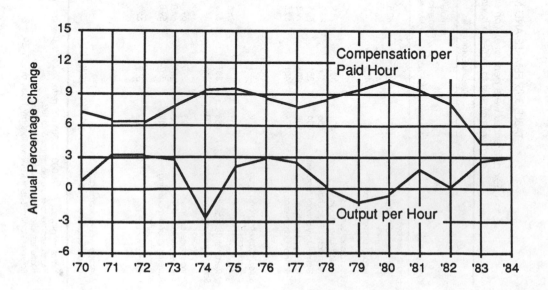

Source: *Statistical Abstract of the United States, 1986,* p. 416.

TABLE 3.17. MEDIAN WEEKLY EARNINGS OF FULL-TIME UNION WORKERS, BY RACE AND GENDER, IN RELATIONSHIP TO NONUNION EARNINGS, 1985

Union members earn more than nonunion workers in all groups shown.

Category	Median Earnings		Union-Nonunion Ratio	
	Men	Women	Men	Women
White, All workers	$417	$281	114.1	127.8
Union members	476	359		
Black, All workers	304	252	126.6	127.0
Union members	385	320		
Hispanic origin,				
All workers	295	229	133.9	124.9
Union members	395	286		

Source: *Employment & Earnings* (January 1986), pp. 210, 215.

FIGURE 3.3. UNION MEMBERS AS PERCENTAGE OF PRODUCTION WORKERS, 1961 AND 1984

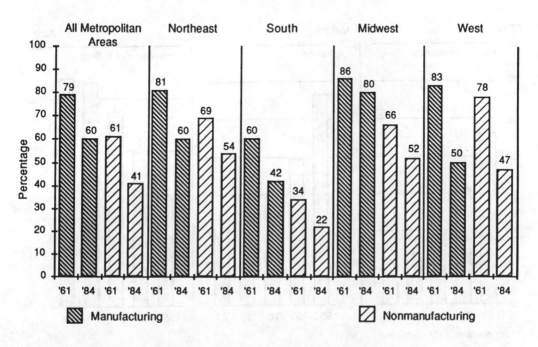

Source: *Monthly Labor Review* (Washington, D.C., September 1985), p. 15.

TABLE 3.18. FEDERAL AND STATE SAFETY AND HEALTH INSPECTIONS, 1976–1983

The number of inspections declined by 42 percent during this period, and the number of employees covered declined by 51 percent.

	Number of Establishments Inspected			Number of Employees Covered by Inspections (in thousands)		
	Federal	State	Total	Federal	State	Total
1976	90,482	166,612	257,094	6,601.7	7,078.3	13,680.0
1978	52,278	122,761	175,039	4,522.6	5,739.6	10,262.2
1980	63,404	106,091	169,595	3,691.0	4,340.3	8,031.3
1983	52,818	103,879	156,697	2,925.0	3,818.3	6,743.3

Source: *Preventing Illness and Injury in the Workplace, 1985*, p. 366.

FIGURE 3.4. CHANGES IN FARMING, 1950–1984

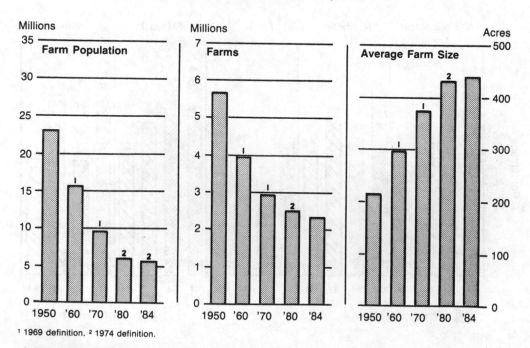

[1] 1969 definition. [2] 1974 definition.

Source: *Statistical Abstract of the United States, 1986*, p. 630.

SECTION 4. GOVERNMENT REVENUES AND EXPENDITURES

In the early and mid-1980s, federal outlays approached $1 trillion. Total outlays (including social insurance) reached a level of 24.7 percent of GNP in 1983, the highest level since World War II. Federal tax receipts rose more slowly; federal deficits after fiscal 1981 were at all-time highs. Federal income tax receipts fell between 1981 and 1983, the first two-year decline ever. State and local government spending neared the $600 billion level in the mid-1980s. Overall, states raise more than they spend; the reverse is true for local governments.

State and local government spending categories shifted somewhat after 1975; a smaller share went to education and larger shares to public welfare, health care, housing, and community development. At the federal level, military spending and interest on the debt both rose, and the share of spending declined for all other purposes including income security, health, education, training, and employment; the shrinkage in the last category was particularly marked.

The composition of federal taxes from 1965 to 1985 shows the largest increase in payroll taxes for social insurance and the greatest decline in corporate taxes, which reached all-time lows. Taxes paid by the poorest fifth of families rose from 9.7 percent of income in 1979 to 11.9 percent in 1984; for the richest fifth of families, total taxes declined over that period from 31.6 to 31.1 percent of income. The tax burden rose for families at the poverty level. In 1980, taxes less transfer income showed a net tax burden averaging 17 percent for all families, ranging from 26 percent for the top tenth to −116 percent for the bottom tenth.

In the 1982–1985 period, 42 of the 250 largest corporations paid no federal income tax or received tax rebates larger than their tax liability; these included AT&T, Dow Chemical, Boeing, Pepsico, General Dynamics, Texaco, Greyhound, General Mills, DuPont, Xerox, and W. R. Grace & Co. For all 250 companies, whose profits totaled $388 billion over this period, the tax rate averaged 14.9 percent. In the 1981–1984 period, the 44 largest nonfinancial corporations with zero or negative tax payments reduced their investment spending on plant and equipment by 4 percent and total employment by 6 percent. In 1985, eleven of these firms spent a total of $39.6 billion merging with or acquiring other corporations. Corporate profits overall reached an all-time high of $286 billion in 1984.

In addition to "tax expenditures"— taxes not imposed as a result of exemptions or deductions provided in the federal tax code—business firms benefit from direct federal expenditures and guarantees, the business equivalent of income or in-kind benefits. In 1986 these direct expenditures were worth $15.7 billion, and subsidized credits were worth an additional $7.6 billion. Major categories included agricultural support, energy research and development, and urban development action grants (UDAGs).

In 5 of the 16 fiscal years between 1969 and 1984, the actual level of federal outlays or receipts varied by 5 percent or more from official estimates. Department of Defense projections seem to be particularly unreliable. Military spending as a percentage of appropriations was 58.6 percent in fiscal 1980 and 49.9 percent in fiscal 1985; in this period unobligated balances rose from $24.2 billion to $61.5 billion, and total unexpended funds in fiscal 1985 were $244.4 billion.

In 1986, Congress enacted a program of significant tax reform in pursuit of greater fairness and equity in assessment. Although these are important public policy objectives, we need to be mindful as well of the necessity for a revenue base sufficient to carry out the responsibilities only government can meet in a society as complex and dynamic as ours. A nation's decision about how much income to allocate for public purposes and needs is a critical reflection of its capacity to understand and accept its responsibility to promote and safeguard the general welfare. Opportunity and caring are the two linked faces of a society.

TABLE 4.1. GOVERNMENT RECEIPTS AND GNP, 1950–1984

Federal receipts as a share of GNP reached their modern peak in 1981. By 1984 they were at the 1960 level. State and local receipts have been relatively stable since 1970. The 1984 combined share of GNP was the lowest since the 1960s.

Year	Federal (in billions)	State and Local (in billions)	Percentage of GNP		Total Percentage of GNP
			Federal	State and Local	
1950	39.4	16.6	14.9	6.3	21.1
1960	92.5	38.8	18.6	7.8	26.4
1970	192.8	96.9	19.9	10.0	29.9
1975	279.1	157.5	18.9	10.6	29.5
1980	517.1	254.4	20.1	9.9	30.0
1981	599.3	280.2	20.8	9.7	30.5
1982	617.8	303.0	20.3	9.9	30.2
1983	600.6	333.1	18.6	10.3	29.0
1984	666.5	364.9	18.6	10.2	28.8

Source: U.S. Office of Management and Budget, *Budget of the United States, Fiscal Year 1986*, (Washington, D.C.: U.S. Government Printing Office, 1985).

TABLE 4.2. PERCENTAGE DISTRIBUTION OF FEDERAL BUDGET OUTLAYS (EXCLUDING SOCIAL SECURITY AND MEDICARE), 1970–1984

The military share declined in the 1970s and rose sharply between 1980 and 1984. Military and interest payments on the national debt together were 54.9 percent of the total in 1984. All other categories including health and income security were stable or declined after 1980.

Category	1970	1975	1980	1982	1984
National defense	51.3	34.0	30.4	34.1	36.9
Income security	9.8	19.7	19.7	19.8	18.3
Net interest	9.0	9.1	11.9	15.6	18.0
Health	3.7	5.0	5.3	5.0	4.9
Education, training, and employment	5.4	6.2	7.2	4.9	4.5
Veterans	5.4	6.5	4.8	4.4	4.2
Transportation	4.4	4.3	4.8	3.8	3.8
International affairs	2.7	2.8	2.9	2.3	2.6
Agriculture	3.2	1.2	2.0	2.9	2.2
Natural resources	1.9	2.9	3.1	2.4	2.0
All others	3.2	8.3	7.9	4.8	2.8
Total	100.0	100.0	100.0	100.0	100.0
Total (in billions)	$159.2	$254.8	$440.3	$543.2	$616.0

Source: *Budget of the United States, Fiscal Year 1986*, pp. 3.2(4)–3.2(5).

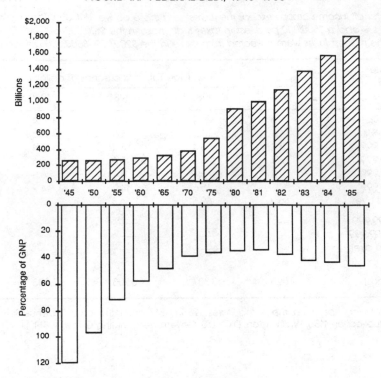

FIGURE 4.1. FEDERAL DEBT, 1945–1985

Source: Data from *Statistical Abstract of the United States, 1986,* p. 305.

TABLE 4.3. PERCENTAGE COMPOSITION OF TAXES, 1950–1985

Corporate taxes showed the largest decline and payroll taxes the largest increase. By 1985 payroll taxes ranked second in total taxes collected, after income taxes.

Year	Individual	Corporation	Social Insurance	Excise	All Other[a]
1950	39.9	26.5	11.0	19.1	3.4
1960	44.0	23.2	15.9	12.6	4.2
1965	41.8	21.8	19.0	12.5	4.9
1970	46.9	17.0	23.0	8.1	4.9
1975	43.9	14.6	30.3	5.9	5.4
1980	47.2	12.5	30.5	4.7	5.1
1981	47.7	12.5	30.5	6.8	4.8
1982	48.2	8.0	32.6	5.9	5.3
1983	48.1	6.2	34.8	5.9	5.0
1984	44.4	8.5	36.3	5.6	5.2
1985	45.6	8.3	36.1	4.9	5.1

[a]Customs, estate, gift, and miscellaneous taxes.
Source: *Budget of the United States Government, Fiscal Year 1986.*

TABLE 4.4. AVERAGE TAX ON TAXABLE INDIVIDUAL INCOME TAX RETURNS, 1975–1983

Taxes fell for all income groups except the lowest and those above $100,000. Those with incomes above $500,000 paid less in taxes than those in the $100,000–500,000 range. The highest taxes were collected from those in the $200,000–$500,000 category in 1983.

Income Group (Adjusted Gross Income)	Average Tax (in thousands of dollars)				
	1975	1980	1981	1982	1983
Under $10,000	.5	.4	.4	.4	.4
$10,000–$19,999	1.6	1.6	1.6	1.6	1.3
$20,000–$29,999	3.4	3.4	3.4	3.4	2.9
$30,000–$39,999	6.7	5.6	5.6	5.6	4.6
$40,000–$49,999	8.4	8.4	8.4	6.8	17.5
$50,000–$99,999		15.6	14.9	14.9	12.2
$100,000 and over	66.2	69.5	66.3	65.7	65.7
$100,000–$199,999	—	—	—	—	35.4
$200,000–$499,999	—	—	—	—	96.4
$500,000 and over	—	—	—	—	44.6
Total Returns (in thousands)	2,025	3,387	3,703	3,603	3,514

Sources: *Statistical Abstract of the United States, 1986*, p. 317; and U.S. Internal Revenue Service, *Statistics of Income* (Publication 1136, Washington, D.C.: U.S. Government Printing Office, 1985), p. 101.

TABLE 4.5. TOTAL INCOME TAX AS PERCENTAGE OF TAXABLE INCOME, 1975–1984

Taxes declined after 1980 as a percentage of income for all groups, most for those with incomes of $100,000 or more.

Income Group	1975	1980	1981	1982	1983	1984	Change 1980–1983	Change 1980–1984
Under $10,000	15.0	8.4	8.2	7.6	6.9	6.0[a]	−1.5	—
$10,000–$19,999	17.6	13.7	13.7	12.3	11.2	7.5[b]	−2.5	—
$20,000–$29,999	20.2	17.0	17.2	15.8	14.4	13.5[c]	−2.6	—
$30,000–$39,999	24.4	20.1	20.2	18.3	16.7	15.9	—	−4.2
$40,000–$49,999		23.5	23.4	21.2	19.2	18.4	—	−5.1
$50,000–$99,999	33.3	29.9	29.3	26.9	24.4	23.2	—	−6.7
$100,000 and over	47.8	46.6	45.6	41.6	40.2	39.3	—	−7.3
Total	21.1	20.0	20.5	18.8	18.1	17.7	−3.0	−3.4

[a]Under $11,000.
[b]$11,000–$18,999.
[c]$19,000–$29,999.

Sources: *Statistical Abstract of the United States, 1986*, p. 317; *Statistics of Income* (Spring 1986) 5 (4), p. 103.

FIGURE 4.2 TAX BURDEN OF POOR FAMILIES, 1978–1986

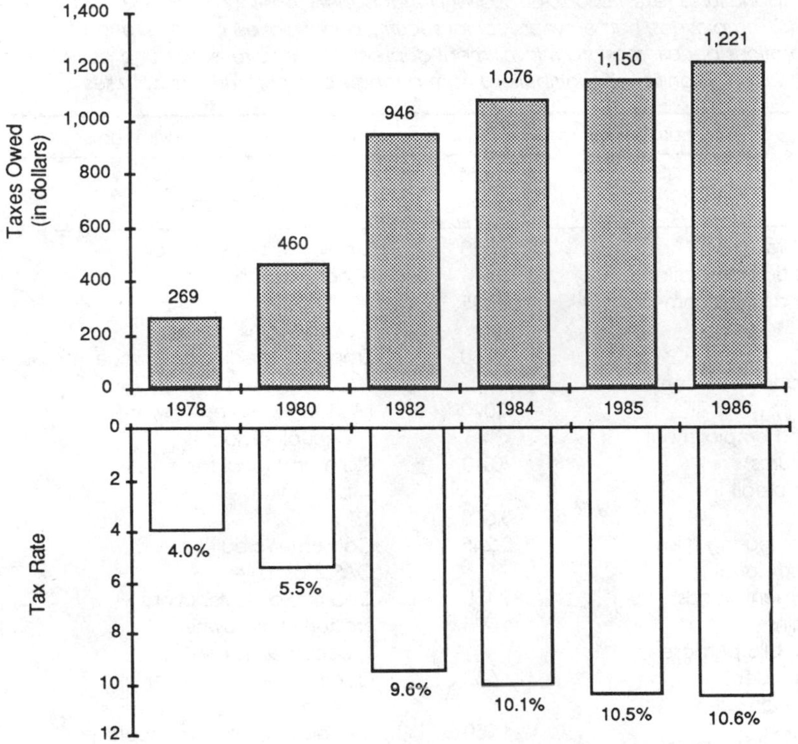

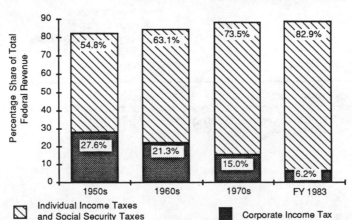

Source: Data from Center on Budget and Policy Priorities, *End Results: The Impact of Federal Policies Since 1980 on Low Income Americans* (Washington, D.C.: Author, 1984), p. 10.

FIGURE 4.3. DECLINING CORPORATE SHARE OF FEDERAL TAXES, 1950–1983

Source: Data from *End Results*, p. 11.

TABLE 4.6. MAJOR TAX EXPENDITURES, FISCAL YEAR 1986

Tax expenditures (exemptions, deductions) that benefit individuals provide major tax relief to employees, homeowners, social security beneficiaries, investors, and others. Corporations benefit most from investment depreciation and research and development, with significant contributions from a range of other business activities.

Corporations		Individuals	
Category	Amount (in millions)	Category	Amount (in millions)
Investment tax credit	$30,520	Employee pension plan contributions	$78,190
Accelerated depreciation			
Machinery and equipment	20,345	Capital gains	42,715
Buildings	6,460	Employer medical insurance contributions	31,285
Research and development expenditures	4,020	Mortgage interest—owner-occupied homes	27,180
Training and employment expenditures	4,010	State and local tax deduction	23,365
Investment credit for ESOPs[a]	3,660	IRAs	21,090
Safe harbor leasing rules	2,245	Consumer credit interest	17,775
Interest—individual development bonds	2,155	OASDI benefits	18,600
Capital gains	1,695	Charitable contributions	11,965
Interest—public purpose state/local debt	1,660	Property tax—owner-occupied house	10,145
Income foreign sales corporation	1,550	Capital gains carryover at death	7,690
Life insurance companies' deduction	7,420	Two-earner married couple deduction	7,420
income deductions	1,425	Interest—state and local public-purpose debt	6,635
Interest—pollution control bonds	1,405	Interest—life insurance, savings	5,370
Income—U.S. possessions	3,040	Investment tax credit structures, etc.	4,580
All other	13,930	Child and dependent care expense	4,020
		All other	48,445

[a]Employee stock option plans.
Source: U.S. Office of Management and Budget, *Budget of the United States Government, Fiscal Year 1987* (Washington, D.C.: U.S. Government Printing Office, 1986).

TABLE 4.7. TAX EXPENDITURE BENEFITS BY INCOME CLASS, 1981–1982

People with incomes above $200,000 benefitted most from tax expenditures; those in the $30,000–50,000 class ranked second: deductions for home ownership and state and local taxes helped this group the most.

Income Class[a]	Owner-Occupied Homes		Capital Gains (in millions)	State and Local Tax Deduction (in millions)	Charitable Contributions (in millions)	Medical Expenses (in millions)	Other (in millions)	Total[b] (in millions)
	Mortgage Interest (in millions)	Property Tax (in millions)						
Less than $10,000	$220	$109	$428	$118	$36	$85	$1,239	$2,235
10,000–15,000	343	198	384	230	129	190	1,153	2,456
15,000–20,000	892	374	308	497	249	299	661	3,280
20,000–30,000	3,633	1,429	1,140	2,276	985	827	1,764	12,054
30,000–50,000	8,639	3,252	2,564	6,289	2,550	1,201	2,316	26,811
50,000–100,000	4,672	2,291	3,179	5,050	2,109	614	1,847	19,762
100,000–200,000	979	725	2,148	2,032	1,126	150	850	8,010
200,000 and over	225	302	3,081	1,352	1,652	56	60,618	67,286
Total	19,602	8,679	13,231	17,844	8,836	3,422	70,448	—

[a]Adjusted gross income; 1982 law, 1981 income levels.
[b]Totals include these other categories, which are not broken down by income class: child and dependent care ($1,314); additional exemption for the elderly ($2,131); investment credit ($3,439); income earned abroad ($930); residential energy credit ($614); dividend exclusion ($506).

Source: U.S. Office of Management and Budget, *Tax Expenditure*; Budget Control Options and Five-Year Budget Projections for Fiscal Years 1983–1987 (Washington, D.C.: U.S. Government Printing Office, November 1982), Table E 1.

TABLE 4.8.   FEDERAL INDIVIDUAL INCOME TAX—EFFECTIVE (AVERAGE) TAX RATES FOR
SELECTED INCOME GROUPS, 1954–1985 (PERCENTAGE)

*Taxes paid as a percentage of income fell moderately between 1965 and 1975, sharply after 1975.
Declines were greatest for those in the highest and lowest groups.*

Adjusted Gross Income in Current Dollars	1954–1963	1965	1970	1975	1985
Single person, no dependents					
$5,000	16.4	13.4	13.7	8.1	3.5
$10,000	21.0	17.4	17.3	14.8	8.9
$20,000	29.5	24.6	22.0	20.6	14.3
$25,000	33.3	27.9	24.4	23.5	16.5
$35,000	39.4	33.2	28.7	27.7	19.8
$50,000	45.6	38.5	34.5	33.4	24.1
$75,000	52.9	44.3	42.1	40.9	29.6
Married couple, two dependents					
$5,000	8.4	5.8	5.8	6.0	−11.0
$10,000	13.7	11.1	11.2	7.1	1.3
$20,000	19.0	15.8	16.1	13.7	8.4
$25,000	21.3	17.6	18.0	16.4	10.3
$35,000	25.8	21.5	21.9	20.5	14.0
$50,000	32.0	26.8	27.3	26.0	18.2
$75,000	39.5	33.4	34.1	32.8	23.5

Source: *Statistical Abstract of the United States, 1986*, p. 319.

TABLE 4.9.   STATE AND LOCAL GOVERNMENTS, SUMMARY OF FINANCE, 1970–1983
(PERCENTAGE)

*Expenditure categories were generally stable. Education declined and health care rose,
as did interest payments. Public welfare rose only modestly.*

Category	1970	1975	1980	1983
Direct general expenditures	100.0	100.0	100.0	100.0
Education	40.1	38.2	36.3	35.3
Public welfare	11.1	11.9	12.4	12.6
Health and hospitals	7.4	8.2	8.8	9.5
Police protection and correction	4.6	5.2	5.4	6.0
Natural resources, parks, and recreation	3.5	3.3	4.8	3.3
Sanitation and sewerage	2.6	3.2	3.2	3.4
Housing and community development	1.7	1.5	1.7	1.8
Interest on general debt	3.4	3.8	4.0	5.2
Other[a]	25.4	24.7	23.4	23.0

[a]Libraries, social insurance administration, veterans' services, highways, airports, water transport,
parking facilities, fire protection, protective inspection and regulation, general control, financial administration, general public buildings, and other and unallocable.
Source: *Statistical Abstract of the United States, 1986*, p. 271.

FIGURE 4.4. AVERAGE TAX RATE AND AVERAGE TOTAL INCOME TAX, 1979–1983

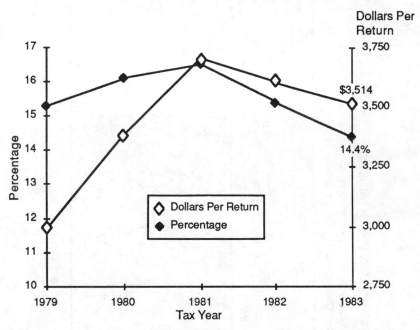

Source: Data from U.S. Internal Revenue Service, *Statistics of Income Bulletin* (Washington, D.C.: Author, Winter 1986), p. 42.

TABLE 4.10. ELEVEN LARGEST CITIES, SOURCES OF REVENUE, 1983

New York exceeds any other city by almost seven times in all categories. All these cities—some much more than others—rely on support from the federal government and from their state governments.

Cities Ranked by Population Size (1980 Census)	Total Revenue[a] (in millions)	Received From			Debt (in millions)
		Taxes (in millions)	Federal Government (in millions)	State and Local Government (in millions)	
New York[b]	$22,569	$8,654.7	$1,303.3	$6,723.8	$11,491
Chicago	2,496	1,017.1	485.0	258.3	1,233
Los Angeles	3,415	858.2	237.1	129.2	3,117
Philadelphia[b]	2,527	951.3	286.5	285.6	2,296
Houston	1,206	535.1	108.8	20.4	1,821
Detroit	1,642	453.1	383.5	307.3	923
Baltimore[b]	1,531	391.3	108.9	700.1	1,005
San Francisco[b]	1,832	480.7	193.5	391.7	1,104
Memphis	1,341	149.8	103.2	257.4	602
Washington, D.C.[b]	2,634	1,328.5	823.3	14.4	1,999
Boston	1,078	355.0	84.9	398.7	597

[a]Includes categories not shown separately.
[b]Represents, in effect, city-county consolidated government.
Source: *Statistical Abstract of the United States, 1986*, p. 290.

TABLE 4.11. ELEVEN LARGEST CITIES, EXPENDITURES, 1983 (IN MILLIONS)

New York has by far the highest welfare, health care, and community development burden of any city shown. States pay all of the education and welfare expenditures for some of these cities.

Cities Ranked by Population Size (1980 Census)	Total Expenditures[a]	General Expenditure								Utility Expenditures
		Total	Education	Highways	Public Welfare	Health and Hospitals	Police Protection	Fire Protection	Community Development	
New York	$20,434	$16,412	$3,609.7	$457.8	$3,530.7	$1,769.7	$933.0	$474.9	$1,023.2	$2,547
Chicago	2,360	2,087	22.4	149.5	64.3	53.1	429.5	150.6	124.9	104
Los Angeles	3,132	1,673	—	56.1	—	.6	330.5	142.8	117.4	1,128
Philadelphia	2,536	1,821	45.4	56.1	77.6	123.4	232.9	79.5	153.9	578
Houston	1,251	1,066	—	74.9	—	32.6	158.4	124.1	14.5	152
Detroit	1,652	1,283	4.7	110.4	—	65.2	190.6	61.1	123.2	206
Baltimore	1,335	1,262	347.5	251.7	.7	117.7	96.1	53.9	28.0	32
San Francisco	1,566	1,141	27.0	6.1	139.1	199.0	98.4	56.7	47.9	299
Memphis	1,232	545	226.7	26.3	.1	9.8	49.1	37.0	22.1	656
Washington, D.C.	2,659	2,337	426.9	68.5	375.2	229.9	157.9	52.4	120.6	64
Boston	1,004	848	254.2	17.8	5.5	100.7	66.4	51.1	43.6	25

[a]Includes categories not shown.
Source: *Statistical Abstract of the United States, 1986,* p. 291.

SECTION 5. SOCIAL WELFARE EXPENDITURES, PROGRAMS, AND RECIPIENTS

Total social welfare spending has risen steadily but unevenly. Between 1975 and 1983, spending for social insurance programs, supported by their own tax and trust fund structures, rose by 168.8 percent and all other social welfare spending rose by 86.3 percent—half as fast. By several measures, the imbalance between the level of need and the provision of benefits to those who need them has increased. Social insurance programs themselves show a mixed record—coverage and benefits have increased for OASI (Old Age and Survivors' Insurance) beneficiaries; coverage of disabled workers was cut substantially between 1981 and 1983 before extensive litigation followed by congressional action slowed the cuts. Between 1980 and 1981, the number of claims denied doubled; between 1980 and 1984, terminations increased from 1,431 to 25,681; between 1978 and 1983 the number of beneficiaries declined by 21.7 percent.

At a time when unemployment rates reached and remained at new postwar highs, unemployment insurance covered an ever-decreasing share of the unemployed. Means-tested programs, including Aid to Families with Dependent Children (AFDC) and food stamps, show declining levels of expenditure, coverage, and benefits; Supplemental Security Income (SSI) coverage was lower in 1984 than in the 1975–1980 period. The share of all children receiving AFDC rose from 9 percent in 1970 to 12 percent in 1980 and fell to 11 percent in 1982; changes in federal AFDC standards adopted in 1981 reduced eligibility.

Many people receive one or more social welfare benefits. In 1984–1985, the Census Bureau put the number at 47 percent of households, or 31 percent of the population. Thirty-seven percent of households receive non-means-tested benefits, predominantly social security and Medicare; 19 percent receive means-tested benefits including food stamps (8.3 percent) and Medicaid (7.8 percent). AFDC and SSI are the income support programs and Medicaid the in-kind program that involve significant state and local spending. In fiscal 1983 the state-local share was 33.3 percent of the income support and 43 percent of the medical care programs. In several states, part of the state share is borne by local governments; in most the state pays all of the nonfederal share.

Before 1982 the coverage of in-kind benefits—food and nutrition, health care, and housing—rose when the poverty rate rose; after 1981 this trend was reversed. In 1982, 40 percent of poor households received none of these benefits. In the 1982 recession, when the poverty rate rose, the number of households receiving means-tested benefits declined slightly to 14.6 million; food stamp and school lunch recipients rose; Medicaid recipients declined. In that year Medicaid reached 39 percent of all poor households and half of poor households with children under 19. Food stamps reached 31 percent of female-headed households, 26 percent of black households, and 19 percent of Hispanic households.

Medicaid (21.5 million recipients) and food stamps (19.8 million recipients) have the broadest reach of means-tested programs; coverage of both was cut after 1980. School meals (11.6 million recipients) and housing assistance (9.3 million recipients) reach fewer people. Means-tested income support programs measured as a percentage of GNP peaked in 1975 and declined thereafter, reaching new lows after 1983. The effect of the legislative changes enacted in 1981 was to reduce expenditures for social welfare 8.8 percent between fiscal 1981 and 1984; major cuts included food stamps (down $2.3 billion) and child nutrition programs (down $1.4 billion); Medicaid expenditures rose.

Unemployment insurance covered a smaller share of the unemployed in the 1980s than in prior years. Recipients tended to be older, more often male and white, with somewhat higher family incomes than the unemployed as a whole, and more of them were employed in construction, mining, and manufacturing and fewer in service industries. Benefit levels in 1983 averaged $119 per week, with a range from $130 or more in fifteen jurisdictions to $85–$100 in thirteen. Puerto Rico paid the lowest benefits ($63). Average benefits in 1985 were 35 percent of average wages.

Child support enforcement and compensatory education programs affected the largest number of children among child-focused education and social welfare service programs in fiscal 1985.

About one in four people in female-headed families were AFDC recipients between 1950 and 1965; by 1971–1972, the share had increased to more than half. After the mid-1970s the number of female-headed families increased faster than AFDC enrollment. Half of AFDC enrollments last less than two years; about 15 percent last eight years or longer. In 1983 the median number of months of AFDC was 26, lower than in previous years. People most frequently apply for AFDC because of an event that creates a female-headed family with children; people most frequently leave AFDC because of marriage, because a child reaches 18, or because their level of earnings is above the eligibility threshold.

In 1984, 33 jurisdictions increased AFDC payments and in 1985, 38 did—27 of them by $15 or more per month. As a result the median state benefit for a family of four rose from $379 to $399, the first increase in real terms since 1976. The number of recipients in 1985 was at the midpoint of the range between 1972 and 1985. Between 1975 and 1983, the share represented by working mothers had dropped substantially, as had the percentage of families with earnings, reflecting the 1981 changes in the law that limited or eliminated the ability to work and to qualify for AFDC benefits. The percentage relying wholly on AFDC for income was 86.8, above previous years. The average family size was 3.0 persons, similar to that of previous years. Forty-three percent of recipients were black, 42 percent white, and 12 percent Hispanic, little changed from prior years. Relatively fewer recipients lived in public housing than in prior years, and more were receiving food stamps—83 percent in 1983. In 1984, 246,337 families with 1,074,170 recipients in 26 jurisdictions were in the AFDC-UP (unemployed parent) program. Permanent exit from AFDC into self-sufficiency depends on opportunities for employment at decent wage levels and on the stability of families—itself in large measure a function of labor market conditions.

There has been dissatisfaction with the official poverty statistics and standards virtually from the time they were first used; to our knowledge, the United States is the only country with such an official measure. If one adjusts the official standard in various ways, the level of poverty varies; these adjustments include, for example, using after-tax rather than total income and pricing noncash benefits in various ways. For 1982, these various calculations yield estimates ranging from a low of 28.7 million to a high of 37.6 million, and a poverty rate ranging from 12.5 to 16.4 percent. All agree, however, that between 1980 and 1982 the number of poor people increased by between 5.1 and 6.2 million, and that the rate rose by between 2.0 and 2.7 percent. All agree that poverty is most severe among female-headed households, blacks, and Hispanics. One analysis indicates that the effectiveness of means-tested antipoverty programs diminished substantially between 1979 and 1984, particularly for families with children. For all such families, the distribution of income became increasingly unequal between 1968 and 1984; the share of the lowest fifth dropped from 7.5 percent in 1968 to 4.6 percent in 1984, and average cash income in constant (1984) dollars dropped from $10,254 to $6,262. Declining earnings, increases in single parenthood, and increased tax burdens together produced this outcome.

Analysts at the Institute for Research on Poverty at the University of Wisconsin concluded that—with both cash and in-kind means-tested benefits growing smaller and losing their antipoverty effectiveness—social insurance had proved by far the most effective instrument for reducing poverty over the 1965–1983 period. For 1983 they estimated that these programs helped 78 percent of whites and 50 percent of nonwhites 65 and over and 14 percent of white women with children and 8 percent of nonwhite women with children to leave poverty.

By 1984 federal expenditures on education had reached $19 billion, $3 billion represented by Title I of the Elementary and Secondary Education Act, serving 4.7 million children in school. The Higher Education Act provides support to college and graduate students at a level of $13 billion per year. Until 1985, Congress successfully resisted efforts to cut these programs. The bulk of education expenditures at the elementary and secondary levels are paid by the states. Between 1971–1972 and 1980–1981, total spending more than doubled, and the share paid by the states rose over most of this period. In many states, increased state spending has brought with it greater regulation.

The United States is unique among industrialized countries in its dual system of social welfare—a public system for some and a private system for those who qualify through their employment. In 1980, these private benefits were estimated at $435 billion, equal to 32.3 percent of wages and salaries. They provide pension, medical care, dental, psychiatric, and other benefits to those who are enrolled; they exclude many of the aged as well as the unemployed and many of the working poor. One of the links between the systems is the process of educating, training, and placing new job seekers, the unemployed, and others. These programs were cut substantially after 1981; for fiscal 1985, federal expenditures and tax credits totaled $6.2 billion and reached about 9 million people, of whom 5 million were employed people who benefited from the dependent care tax credit.

Hunger is a problem whose existence is clear but whose scope and direction resist quantification. Studies sponsored in 1977 and 1979 by the Field Foundation, research by the National Centers for Disease Control and the National Center for Health Statistics, and more recent studies sponsored by the Harvard University School of Public Health all testify to continuing interest and continuing controversy. A 1986 study by the Harvard group estimated that fewer than one-third of eligible people in 150 counties afflicted with serious hunger and malnutrition were receiving food stamps and that the total number of recipients had dropped from 65 percent of those eligible in 1980 to 55 percent in 1984. Their 1985 study described hunger as an "epidemic" affecting up to 20 million people who are hungry at least some of the time each month; in this number they included 15.5 million officially poor people who do not qualify for food stamps and about 4.5 million "near poor." In support of their conclusion, they called attention to massive increases in food kitchens and food banks, increased reports of nutrition-related illnesses, cuts in food and nutrition programs, and concrete field reports.

We see a considerable social welfare expenditure that has provided significant benefits and protection to many but has treated sizable groups less generously and fairly. As the nature of poverty has changed, programs to alleviate its burdens have failed to keep pace and attempts to prevent or limit its scope and level have proved ineffective. After many years of national discussion and debate, our society still lacks a coherent set of social welfare policies and programs; our patchwork approach becomes steadily more threadbare. Survey data consistently report significant majorities who support government action to improve the well-being and prospects of the disadvantaged and victimized, but the political response is deficient. The outcomes we report here do not provide grounds for either satisfaction or optimism.

TABLE 5.1. PUBLIC SOCIAL WELFARE EXPENDITURES, 1950–1983 (IN BILLIONS)

Overall expenditures showed continued high growth; social insurance grew almost sixfold between 1970 and 1979; public aid grew fourfold. From 1980 to 1983, total spending rose by 30 percent; social insurance spending was up 44 percent, health care 30 percent, public aid 20 percent.

Category	1950	1960	1970	1975	1979	1980	1983
Total	$23.5	$52.3	$145.9	$290.0	$430.03	$493.2	$641.7
Social insurance	4.9	19.3	54.7	123.0	194.3	229.8	330.6
OASDHI	0.8	11.0	36.8	78.4	131.7	152.1	224.7
Public employee retirement	0.8	2.6	8.7	20.1	33.9	39.5	54.8
Unemployment insurance-employment service	2.2	2.8	3.8	13.8	11.3	18.3	25.3
Workers' compensation	0.6	1.3	3.0	6.5	11.6	13.5	17.39
Medicare	—	—	7.1	14.8	29.1	34.9	56.9
Other	0.5	1.6	3.7	10.6	23.6	—	—
Public aid	2.5	4.1	16.5	41.3	64.6	71.8	85.8
Public assistance[a]	2.5	4.0	14.4	27.4	40.7	44.9	56.6
Supplemental Security Income	—	—	—	6.1	7.5	8.2	10.8
Food stamps	—	—	0.6	4.7	6.5	9.1	11.7
Other	—	0.1	1.5	3.2	9.9	9.6	6.7
Health and medical programs[b]	2.1	4.5	9.9	17.8	24.9	28.3	36.9
Veterans' programs	6.9	5.5	9.1	17.0	20.5	21.5	25.8
Education	6.7	17.6	50.8	80.8	108.3	121.0	141.5
Housing	0.0	0.2	0.7	3.2	6.2	7.2	9.1

[a]Cash and medical payments under the Social Security Act and state and local general assistance.
[b]Excludes Medicaid.
Sources: U.S. Social Security Administration, *Social Security Bulletin, Annual Statistical Supplement, 1984–85* (Baltimore, Md.: Author, 1985), p. 65; and *Social Security Bulletin*, February 1986, pp. 13–16.

TABLE 5.2 SOCIAL SECURITY TRUST FUNDS, 1970–1985 (IN BILLIONS)

The OASI trust fund balances are the largest and show the greatest variation. All balances rose between 1981–1982 and 1985.

Year	Old Age and Survivors' Insurance			Hospital Insurance			Disability Trust Fund		
	Receipts	Expendi-tures	Total End-of-Year Assets	Receipts	Expendi-tures	Total End-of-Year Assets	Receipts	Expendi-tures	Total End-of-Year Assets
1970	$33.2	$29.8	$32.5	$6.0	$5.3	$3.2	$4.9	$3.3	$5.6
1975	59.9	60.4	37.0	12.3	11.6	10.5	7.9	8.8	7.4
1977	72.4	75.6	32.5	15.1	13.7	10.4	9.5	11.9	3.4
1979	90.3	93.1	24.7	21.9	21.1	13.2	15.6	14.2	5.6
1980	105.9	107.6	22.8	25.0	25.6	13.7	13.9	15.9	3.6
1981	125.4	126.7	21.5	34.1	30.7	18.7	17.1	17.7	3.0
1982	125.2	142.1	22.1	36.0	36.1	8.2	22.7	18.0	2.7
1983	150.6	152.9	19.8	41.3	39.9	12.9	20.8	18.2	3.2
1984	169.3	161.9	27.1	43.6	43.9	15.7	17.3	18.5	4.0
1985	184.3	169.6	35.8	48.0	48.4	20.5	19.3	19.5	6.3

Source: *Social Security Bulletin* (April 1986), pp. 31–33.

TABLE 5.3. MAXIMUM TAXABLE EARNINGS, CONTRIBUTION RATES AND MAXIMUM TAX, SOCIAL SECURITY, 1937–1986

The combination of rising tax rates and maximum taxable earnings lifted the maximum tax 212 percent between 1966 and 1976, and a further 236 percent between 1976 and 1986, when the maximum tax was 100 times its 1937 level.

Year	Annual Maximum Taxable Earnings	Contribution Rate Total (percentage)	Maximum Tax	Year	Annual Maximum Taxable Earnings	Contribution Rate Total (percentage)	Maximum Tax
1937	$3,000	1.0	$30.00	1971	7,800	5.2	405.60
1950	3,000	1.5	45.00	1972	9,000	5.2	468.00
1951	3,600	1.5	54.00	1973	10,800	5.9	631.80
1954	3,600	2.0	72.00	1974	13,200	5.9	772.20
1955	4,200	2.0	84.00	1975	14,100	5.9	824.85
1957	4,200	2.3	94.50	1976	15,300	5.9	895.05
1959	4,800	2.5	120.00	1977	16,500	5.9	965.25
1960	4,800	3.0	144.00	1978	17,700	6.1	1,070.85
1962	4,800	3.1	150.00	1979	22,900	6.1	1,403.77
1963	4,800	3.6	174.00	1980	25,900	6.1	1,587.67
1966	6,600	4.2	277.20	1981	29,700	6.7	1,975.05
1967	6,600	4.4	290.40	1982	32,400	6.7	2,170.80
1968	7,800	4.4	343.20	1983	35,700	6.7	2,391.90
1969	7,800	4.8	374.40	1984	37,800	7.0	2,646.00
1970	7,800	4.8	374.40	1985	39,600	7.1	2,791.80
				1986	42,000	7.2	3,003.00

Sources: *Social Security Bulletin, Annual Statistical Supplement, 1984–85,* pp. 23, 26; and U.S. Social Security Administration, unpublished data (Baltimore, Md.).

TABLE 5.4. WORKERS AND TAXABLE EARNINGS UNDER SOCIAL SECURITY, 1937–1985

Coverage and earnings grew consistently, earnings more rapidly as a result of inflation and increases in maximum taxable earnings.

Year	Number of Workers (in thousands)	Reported Taxable Earnings (in billions)	Average Annual Earnings per Worker
1937	32,900	$29.6	$761
1950	48,280	87.5	1,926
1960	72,530	207.0	2,833
1970	93,090	415.6	4,317
1975	100,200	664.7	5,790
1978	110,600	915.8	7,204
1980	113,300	1,174.7	8,612
1982	112,600	1,363.4	10,083
1983	113,400	1,453.0	10,455
1984	118,500	1,604.8	—
1985	121,600	1,707.3	—

Sources: *Social Security Bulletin, Annual Statistical Supplement, 1984–85,* p. 83; and U.S. Social Security Administration, unpublished data (Baltimore, Md.).

TABLE 5.5. SOCIAL WELFARE EXPENDITURES AS PERCENTAGE OF GROSS NATIONAL PRODUCT (GNP) 1950–1983

Social welfare spending increased until 1975, declined thereafter, and rose after 1980. More than seven-tenths of expenditures were represented by social insurance and education.

Category	1950	1960	1970	1975	1979	1980	1983
Social insurance	1.7	3.8	5.5	7.9	8.0	8.7	10.0
Public aid	0.9	0.8	1.7	2.7	2.7	2.7	2.6
Health and medical programs	0.7	0.9	1.0	1.2	1.0	1.1	1.1
Veterans' programs	2.4	1.1	0.9	1.1	0.8	0.8	0.8
Education	2.3	3.5	5.1	5.2	4.5	4.6	4.3
Other social welfare	0.1	0.2	0.4	0.4	0.5	0.5	0.4
Total	8.2	10.3	14.7	18.7	17.8	18.7	19.4

Source: *Social Security Bulletin* (February 1986), p. 17.

TABLE 5.6. AVERAGE MONTHLY PAYMENTS, SELECTED PUBLIC ASSISTANCE PROGRAMS, 1960–1985[a]

Significant differences exist and persist among different categories of beneficiaries; OASDHI beneficiaries received rising real incomes while those of the aged and disabled rose slightly and fell for AFDC recipients.

Program	1960	1970	1975	1980	1981	1984	1985
OASDHI, all retired workers	$261.59	$312.85	$393.06	$416.84	$432.59	$460.57	$478.62
OASDHI, widowed mother with two children	664.21	771.13	891.48	942.59	961.63	986.02	—
Old Age Assistance (until 1970)	208.10	205.70	—	—	—	—	—
Supplemental Security Income (after 1974)	—	—	172.45	156.45	154.45	157.88	—
Aid to Families with Dependent Children (AFDC) per recipient	100.16	133.25	132.21	118.56	115.61	114.56	—

[a]All figures for December of the years cited in real (1984) dollars.
Sources: *Social Security Bulletin, Annual Statistical Supplement, 1984–85*, p. 234; and *Social Security Bulletin* (April 1986), p. 39.

TABLE 5.7. PERCENTAGE OF THE UNEMPLOYED RECEIVING UNEMPLOYMENT INSURANCE BENEFITS, 1967–1985

The share of unemployed receiving this benefit reached a peak in the 1975–1976 recession and hit a new low in 1985.

Year	Percentage Covered	Average Monthly Number Not Receiving Benefits (in thousands)	Unemployment Rates (percentage)
1967	43	1,696	3.8
1968	42	1,634	3.6
1969	41	1,671	3.5
1970	48	2,128	4.9
1971	52	2,408	5.9
1972	45	2,685	5.6
1973	41	2,575	4.9
1974	50	2,578	5.6
1975	76	1,903	8.5
1976	67	2,444	7.7
1977	56	3,076	7.1
1978	43	3,535	6.1
1979	42	3,559	5.8
1980	50	3,819	7.1
1981	41	4,881	7.6
1982	45	5,873	9.7
1983	44	6,002	9.6
1984	34	5,636	7.5
1985	33	5,602	7.2

Source: Center on Budget and Policy Priorities, unpublished data (Washington, D.C., 1986).

TABLE 5.8. POVERTY THRESHOLDS FOR NONFARM FAMILIES, 1960–1986[a]

Criteria of poverty measurement change only to adjust for changes in Consumer Price Index. Separate farm and nonfarm categories were eliminated in 1983. Alaska and Hawaii are calculated separately.

Year	Unrelated Individuals Under Age 65	Two-Person Families, Head Under Age 65	Four-Person Families
1960	$1,526	$1,982	$3,022
1970	2,010	2,604	3,968
1980[b]	4,290	5,537	8,414
1981	4,729	6,111	9,287
1982	5,019	6,487	9,862
1983	5,180	6,697	10,178
1984	5,400	6,983	10,609
1985	5,250	7,050	10,650
1986	5,360	7,240	11,000

[a]Poverty thresholds are derived from the 1964 index devised by the Social Security Administration, adjusted annually for price changes.
[b]Same poverty income thresholds for nonfarm and farm.
Sources: U.S. Social Security Administration, *Social Security Bulletin, Annual Statistical Supplement, 1981* (Baltimore, Md., 1982), p. 59; and *Social Security Bulletin, Annual Statistical Supplement, 1984–85*, p. 70; for 1985–1986 data: *Federal Register* (March 8, 1985, and February 11, 1986).

TABLE 5.9. PERCENTAGE DISTRIBUTION OF MEANS-TESTED NONCASH BENEFIT HOUSEHOLDS BY SELECTED CHARACTERISTICS, 1984

White households account for three-fifths or more of in-kind benefit recipients. Families with children and all female-headed households account for major shares of these benefits. People over 65 are an important group among those living in public housing.

Characteristic	Number Households Receiving Benefits (in thousands)	Food Stamps	Free or Reduced Price School Lunches	Public or Other Subsidized Housing	Medicaid
White	75,328	63.6	61.7	60.9	66.7
Black	9,480	33.5	34.2	36.6	30.3
Hispanic origin[a]	4,881	11.9	17.1	10.1	12.1
Households with					
Children under 19	34,552	65.0	100.0	47.9	52.7
Female householder, no husband present	10,129	41.8	47.4	37.9	38.8
Householder 65 or older	18,155	15.4	3.3	32.2	28.6
Residence in South	29,581	38.4	42.4	34.8	30.3
Total (in thousands)		(7,061)	(5,637)	(3,588)	(8,323)

[a]Persons of Hispanic origin may be of any race.
Source: "Characteristics of Households and Persons Receiving Selected Non-Cash Benefits, 1984," p. 2.

FIGURE 5.1. HOUSEHOLDS RECEIVING MEANS-TESTED BENEFITS, 1984

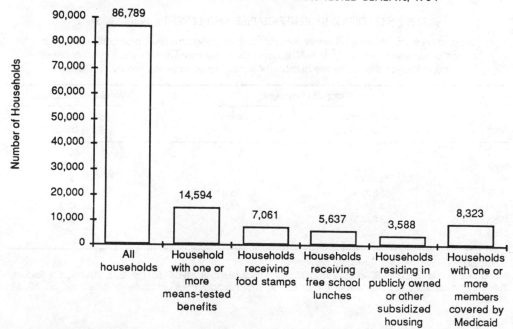

Source: U.S. Bureau of the Census, "Characteristics of Households and Persons Receiving Selected Non-Cash Benefits, 1984," in *Current Population Reports* (Washington, D.C.: Author, 1984), p. 2.

TABLE 5.10. STATES WITH 1,000,000 OR MORE SOCIAL SECURITY BENEFICIARIES, DECEMBER 1984

Half of all beneficiaries live in nine states, most with large and aging industrial economies.

State	Number of Beneficiaries (in thousands)
California	3,319
New York	2,788
Florida	2,243
Pennsylvania	2,118
Texas	1,899
Ohio	1,672
Illinois	1,661
Michigan	1,395
New Jersey	1,169
Nine-state total	18,264
U.S. total	36,414

Source: *Social Security Bulletin, Annual Statistical Supplement, 1984–85,* p. 194.

TABLE 5.11. AID TO FAMILIES WITH DEPENDENT CHILDREN (AFDC), AVERAGE MONTHLY NUMBER OF RECIPIENTS, 1955–1985

AFDC coverage reached a peak in 1975; by 1983 the total number was 4.7 percent less than in 1975. In this same period the number of poor people rose by 9.6 million, or 37 percent.

Year	Recipients (in thousands)		
	Total	Families	Children
1955	2,192	602	1,661
1960	3,073	803	2,370
1965	4,396	1,054	3,316
1970	9,659	2,552	7,033
1975	11,404	3,568	8,106
1980	11,101	3,843	7,599
1981	10,613	3,633	7,125
1982	10,504	3,596	6,972
1983	10,659	3,651	7,051
1984	10,868	3,726	7,155
1985	10,794	3,685	7,163

Source: *Social Security Bulletin* (April, 1986), p. 48.

TABLE 5.12 DISABILITY BENEFICIARIES AND BENEFITS, 1960–1985[a]

Expenditures (mostly federal) under federal disability programs are consistently the major source of disability benefits. Until 1979, expenditures rose more rapidly than the number of beneficiaries; thereafter the number of beneficiaries was reduced by 869,000.

Year	Disability Payments		Workers' Compensation
	Beneficiaries (in thousands)	Benefits (in billions)	Benefits (in billions)
1960	542.6	$0.6	$0.9
1970	2,572.7	0.1	2.0
1975	4,142.1	8.4	4.6
1979	4,822.7	15.4	9.6
1980	4,728.7	17.5	12.2
1983	3,874.9	18.8	13.7
1985	3,907.2	—	—

[a]Excluding payments for remedial care.

Sources: *Social Security Bulletin, Annual Statistical Supplement, 1984–85,* pp. 223, 224; *Social Security Bulletin, Annual Statistical Supplement, 1981,* pp. 66, 67; and *Social Security Bulletin, June 1986,* pp. 35, 38, 39, 42.

TABLE 5.13. CHANGES IN MAXIMUM AFDC BENEFITS FOR A FOUR-PERSON FAMILY,
50 STATES AND DISTRICT OF COLUMBIA, 1970 AND 1985

*Benefits in real (1985) dollars fell over this period in every state
except three—California, Maine, and Wisconsin.*

| State | July 1970 Benefit | January 1985 Benefit | Changes (percentage) | |
			Current Dollars	Constant Dollars
Alabama	$81	$147	81	−33
Alaska	375	800	113	−21
Arizona	167	282	69	−38
Arkansas	100	191	91	−29
California	221	660	199	10
Colorado	235	420	79	−34
Connecticut	330	636	93	−29
Delaware	187	336	80	−34
District of Columbia	238	399	68	−38
Florida	134	284	112	−22
Georgia	133	245	84	−32
Hawaii	263	546	108	−23
Idaho	242	344	42	−48
Illinois	282	368	30	−52
Indiana	150	316	111	−22
Iowa	243	419	72	−36
Kansas	244	422	73	−36
Kentucky	187	246	32	−51
Louisiana	109	234	115	−21
Maine	168	465	177	2
Maryland	190	376	92	−29
Massachusetts	314	463	47	−46
Michigan[a]	263	512	95	−28
Minnesota	299	611	104	−25
Mississippi	70	120	71	−37
Missouri	130	308	137	−13
Montana	228	425	86	−31
Nebraska	200	420	110	−22
Nevada	143	279	95	−28
New Hampshire	294	429	46	−46
New Jersey	347	443	28	−53
New Mexico	182	313	72	−37
New York[b]	336	566	68	−38
North Carolina	158	244	54	−43
North Dakota	261	454	74	−36
Ohio	200	360	80	−34
Oklahoma	185	349	89	−30
Oregon	225	468	108	−23
Pennsylvania	313	444	42	−48
Rhode Island	263	547[c]	108	−23
South Carolina	103	229	122	−18
South Dakota	300	371	24	−54

(Continued on next page)

TABLE 5.13. (continued)

State	July 1970 Benefit	January 1985 Benefit	Changes (percentage)	
			Current Dollars	Constant Dollars
Tennessee	129	168	30	−52
Texas	179	201	12	−59
Utah	212	425	100	−26
Vermont	304	622	105	−24
Virginia	261	379	45	−46
Washington	303	561	85	−32
West Virginia	138	249	80	−33
Wisconsin	217	636	193	8
Wyoming	227	310	37	−50
Median	221	379	81	−33

[a]Michigan data for Detroit only.
[b]New York data for New York City only.
[c]Winter rate (November–April); summer rate, $440 in 1984.
Source: U.S. Congressional Budget Office, *Reducing Poverty Among Children* (Washington, D.C.: U.S. Government Printing Office, May 1985), pp. 52–53.

TABLE 5.14. STATE CASELOADS AND BENEFIT PAYMENTS, AID TO FAMILIES WITH DEPENDENT CHILDREN (AFDC), 1983

Drastic differences prevail in benefit payments by state. Three states with large caseloads are among the ten highest-paying states; others pay substantially less. Lowest payments are in the southern states.

State	Number of Recipients	Average Monthly Payment for Family
States paying $300 or more		
Alaska	11,725	$542.19
California	1,595,414	466.41
Minnesota	142,494	459.11
Wisconsin	273,267	453.92
Vermont	22,330	421.29
Connecticut	128,321	416.12
Hawaii	54,369	405.41
New York	1,099,115	405.13
Washington	147,732	403.04
Michigan	759,301	399.86
Massachusetts	253,054	379.88
Rhode Island	45,207	360.88
Utah	38,577	341.63
Iowa	106,713	327.08
Nebraska	41,902	318.58
Pennsylvania	577,108	315.20

(Continued on next page)

TABLE 5.14. (continued)

State	Number of Recipients	Average Monthly Payment for Family
New Jersey	394,948	312.34
Maine	49,456	313.62
Wyoming	8,083	307.18
Oregon	73,198	305.62
Montana	18,515	304.64
Kansas	41,902	303.72
States paying $175–$300		
Illinois	738,556	289.42
Colorado	86,720	286.72
New Hampshire	18,462	283.88
North Dakota	11,188	283.82
South Dakota	16,725	244.35
Maryland	192,604	265.49
Ohio	652,651	257.73
Oklahoma	74,677	256.56
Idaho	19,001	256.36
Missouri	185,948	241.45
Delaware	192,604	237.46
Virginia	160,486	231.62
Arizona	69,323	218.28
Indiana	165,059	214.17
New Mexico	48,233	202.86
Florida	284,238	195.98
Nevada	12,848	185.40
Kentucky	154,658	183.60
North Carolina	174,642	182.80
Georgia	241,715	180.00
States paying less than $175		
West Virginia	82,084	169.75
Louisiana	204,690	168.28
Arkansas	63,723	127.61
Tennessee	153,728	115.81
Alabama	154,335	110.85
Texas	316,597	135.71
South Carolina	132,815	127.92
Mississippi	153,575	90.88

Source: *Social Security Bulletin, Annual Statistical Supplement 1984–85*, p. 255.

TABLE 5.15. SUPPLEMENTAL SECURITY INCOME (SSI), BENEFICIARIES AND BENEFITS, 1974–1984

SSI coverage has fluctuated modestly; benefits rose steadily but remained low. Sixty percent of SSI recipients in 1985 were disabled, 38 percent age 65 and over.

Year	Beneficiaries (in thousands)			Average Monthly Benefit
	Federal SSI	Supplementation	Total[a]	
December				
1974	—	—	4,027.6	$114.76
1975	3,893.4	1,987.4	4,359.6	116.36
1976	3,799.1	1,912.6	4,285.3	121.53
1977	3,777.9	1,927.3	4,287.0	126.39
1978	3,754.7	1,046.8	4,265.5	131.79
1979	3,687.1	1,941.6	4,202.7	157.87
1980	3,682.4	1,934.3	4,194.3	170.42
1981	3,590.1	1,874.9	4,067.4	185.49
1982	3,473.3	1,798.4	3,908.5	198.87
1983	3,589.5	1,811.6	3,955.8	214.69
1984	3,698.8	1,875.2	4,094.0	221.87

[a]Figures include double counting.
Source: *Social Security Bulletin, Annual Statistical Supplement, 1984–85*, pp. 240, 242.

TABLE 5.16. FOOD STAMP PROGRAM, 1965–1984

Program participants and total expenditures rose steadily to 1981 and declined thereafter.

Year	Number of Persons Participating (in thousands)	Average Monthly Bonus per Person	Annual Bonus Value of Coupons (in millions)
1965	424	$6.39	$32.5
1970	4,340	10.58	550.8
1975	17,063	21.42	4,386.1
1980	21,077	34.34	8,685.5
1981	22,430	39.44	10,616.0
1982	21,716	39.18	10,205.8
1983	21,630	42.98	11,153.9
1984	20,870	42.77	10,710.6

Source: *Social Security Bulletin, Annual Statistical Supplement, 1984–85*, p. 256.

TABLE 5.17. TRANSFER PROGRAM RECIPIENTS AND ESTIMATED NUMBER ELIGIBLE, 1984[a]

The share of eligible people not receiving benefits is highest for SSI; AFDC
shows the highest coverage; food stamp coverage is lower.

Program	Recipients (in thousands)	Number Eligible (in thousands)	Percentage
SSI	4,030	11,830	34.1
AFDC			
Persons	10,774	13,397	80.4
Families	3,686	4,615	79.9
Food stamps	20,870	31,994	65.2

[a]Since 1975, the federally funded transfer income model (TRIM 2) estimates the numbers eligible for specific programs using Current Population Survey data, changes in federal and state regulations and tax liability, and other data.

Sources: R.C. Michel, Urban Institute, unpublished data (Washington, D.C., 1986); and *Social Security Bulletin* (April 1986), p. 39.

TABLE 5.18. PRIVATE PHILANTHROPY: ESTIMATED FUNDS BY SOURCE AND ALLOCATION, SELECTED YEARS, 1955–1984 (IN MILLIONS)[a]

Totals rose by more than 50 percent between 1980 and 1984. Individuals give
the most. Religion gets more than half of all charitable
contributions; education and health care receive about 14 percent each.

Category	1955	1960	1965	1970	1975	1980	1983	1984
Total	$6,660	$9,390	$13,290	$20,750	$29,680	$47,740	$60,390	$74,250
Source								
Individuals	5,710	7,630	10,360	15,920	24,240	39,930	53,850	61,550
Foundations	300	710	1,130	1,900	2,010	2,400	3,450	4,360
Business corporations	415	482	785	797	1,202	2,550	3,100	3,450
Charitable bequests	237	574	1,020	2,130	2,230	2,860	4,520	4,890
Allocation								
Religion	3,330	4,790	6,510	9,300	12,910	22,150	31,030	35,560
Education	733	1,500	2,260	3,240	3,950	6,680	9,040	10,080
Social welfare	1,530	1,410	1,860	2,880	3,140	4,730	6,940	8,010
Health and hospitals	596	1,130	1,460	3,400	4,420	6,490	9,150	10,440
Arts and humanities	199	188	226	623	1,720	2,960	4,080	4,640
Civic and public	75	94	173	415	890	1,360	1,800	2,080
Other	197	282	797	892	2,650	3,370	2,890	3,440

[a]Estimates for sources of funds are based largely on reports of the Internal Revenue Service (IRS) for itemized deductions, corporate profits, and bequests; data are adjusted for nonitemized IRS deductions and after comparison with levels of gross national product, personal income, population, and publicly reported large bequests.

Sources: American Association of Fund Raising Counsel, *Giving USA, 1985* (New York: Author, 1985), and earlier annual reports.

TABLE 5.19. TOP TEN NONPROFIT ORGANIZATIONS
BY TOTAL REVENUE AND TOTAL ASSETS, 1982[a]

*TIAA and CREF—providing pensions and annuities to academic faculty—are together
the largest organizations in the charitable area measured by assets
and revenues. Major hospitals and universities constitute the remainder.*

Name	Total Revenue (in millions)	Name	Total Assets (in millions)
College Retirement Equities Fund	$4,631	Teachers Insurance and Annuity Association of America	$13,519
Teachers Insurance and Annuity Association of America	3,351	College Retirement Equities Fund	12,821
Kaiser Foundation Health Plan	2,116	Harvard College	3,326
Harvard College	1,342	Yale University	1,836
Kaiser Foundation Hospitals	1,123	Stanford University	1,727
University of Chicago	745	Princeton University	1,415
American National Red Cross	722	Shriners Hospital for Crippled Children	1,273
Sisters of Mercy Health Corporation	718	University of Rochester	1,127
Massachusetts Institute of Technology	692	University of Chicago	1,127
Stanford University	664	Duke University	986

[a]These are the top ten organizations that are exempt from federal income tax on most earnings
because of their IRC 501(c)(3) status.
Source: *SOI Bulletin* (Publication 1136, Winter 1985–1986).

FIGURE 5.2. DISTRIBUTION OF CORPORATE CONTRIBUTIONS, 1983

$1278.4 Millions Reported by 471 Companies

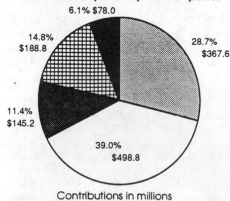

Contributions in millions

Health & Human Services

Education

Civic Activities

Other Activities

Culture & Art

Source: Data from The Conference Board, *Annual Survey of Corporate Contributions* (New York: Author, 1985), p. 11.

TABLE 5.20. TOTAL FUNDS RAISED BY UNITED WAYS IN THE UNITED STATES IN CURRENT AND REAL DOLLARS, 1976–1985

*The amount raised annually has more than
doubled over a ten-year period
in current dollars and for the past two years
has been over $2 billion. Inflation
prevented any gain in real dollars until the
most recent three years.*

Year	Current Dollars (in millions)	1967 Dollars (in millions)
1976	$1,104	$648
1977	1,204	664
1978	1,317	674
1979	1,423	655
1980	1,526	620
1981	1,680	617
1982	1,780	616
1983	1,950	653
1984	2,145	689
1985	2,330	723

Source: United Way of America, special computer runs (Arlington, Va., 1986).

SECTION 6. SOCIAL INDICATORS

In the 1960s and early 1970s, interest among social scientists in ways of quantifying societal well-being helped to stimulate the development of social indicators as a serious enterprise, supported by foundations and ultimately by federal agencies. By the early 1970s, this effort had lost its energy, although the concerns that created it are as relevant now as they were then, and although the work had gone forward in other countries. We include here a variety of tables intended to convey some aspects of our ability to understand and deal with problems that affect the quality of life and people's ability to find shelter, lead crisis-free lives, participate in political and social affairs, raise their level of education, and in other ways achieve their potential. Because one measure of a society is how it deals with its deviants and problem people, and because adherence to decent standards of fairness and equal treatment are important in assessing how well we meet the standards we proclaim, some tables examine the problems of crime, drugs, and prison.

Race remains a major factor in all these areas. In housing, education, homelessness, incarceration, capital punishment, and other areas, the figures for blacks show a consistent pattern of inequality. The percentage of blacks completing high school and college has continued to rise, though unevenly in different geographical regions. Many fewer blacks than whites or Asians study mathematics or science in high school.

A high dropout rate for blacks in high school operates to limit the number applying to or entering college. Differences in funding levels and staff support among urban and suburban schools help to explain different levels of educational achievement between the races. Between 1960 and 1980 the proportion of blacks with some college education tripled and the black-white gap narrowed. By 1984, for the first time, blacks were enrolled in higher education in proportion to their share of the total population.

The National Center for Education Statistics reported that the share of 3- to 5-year-old children enrolled in preschool programs rose between 1970 and 1980 and then declined slightly; enrollments are much higher among children in families with incomes of $20,000 or more and somewhat higher among 5-year-olds from these families as compared with younger children.

Between 1977 and 1982, the number of firms owned by blacks rose by 100,000 (47 percent) to a total of 339,239. Most were small; only 1,129 had receipts of $1 million or more, and 10 percent had one or more paid employees. Seventy percent of all businesses and 95 percent of black businesses were sole proprietorships.

Measures of income in relation to BLS budgetary levels indicate that about one quarter of black families are members of the middle class, a substantially smaller proportion than the white shares, but not insignificant in relation to prior decades. Blacks—both men and women—made modest inroads into upper-level occupations in the 1970s, more so in government than in private employment. The greatest relative gains in income and status were made by young black married couples with both spouses at work. Over both the 1960–1970 and 1970–1980 decades, blacks increased their representation among managers and professionals, college and schoolteachers, lawyers and judges, social scientists, physicians, and social workers, though these occupations still showed a minority of blacks well below the levels for whites.

A 1984 study by the Urban Institute found that except for the elderly the economic condition of blacks had worsened between 1980 and 1984, both in absolute numbers and in relation to the condition of whites. A congressional study in 1984 extended the picture, finding that the economic situation of all families below, at, or near the poverty level had deteriorated over this same period; reduced federal social welfare spending and higher tax burdens were the principal factors producing this outcome.

An Urban Institute study in 1986 focused on "displaced homemakers," whose numbers had increased from 1.7 million women in 1975 to 2.3 million in 1982; they include women between the ages of 35 and 64 who have experienced disruption of their marriage; whose husbands are absent, disabled, or unemployed; or who are about to lose their welfare benefits and who are themselves unemployed, working at jobs that pay below the minimum wage or working fewer hours than they wish to. Marital disruption accounts for about 40 percent of this group; about one-third are married to a disabled or unemployed husband; fewer than one in five are widows. Seventy-seven percent of the group are white and distributed about evenly among age groups. In 1982, more than 40 percent had incomes below $10,000; the mean value was $15,000.

Between 1974 and 1984 the cost of buying a home rose faster than median family income; in May 1984, the median cost was $73,000 compared with $32,000 in 1974, with considerable variation by city and region. High-cost cities included San Diego, San Francisco, Los Angeles, and New York; lower-cost cities included Detroit, Albany, and Tampa. In constant (1976) dollars, average prices rose from $42,200 in 1976 to $53,926 in 1980 and then declined to $51,074 in 1983. Gross rents accounted for 29 percent of family income in 1983 compared with 22 percent in 1973. For low-income families, there were significant increases among those paying 30 percent or more of their incomes in rent, and among those paying more than half of their income in rent, between 1975 and 1983. The share of people living in owner-occupied housing remained stable over the 1960–1983 period. Fewer blacks than whites live in their own homes, and their homes are older on average than the homes of white homeowners. One estimate, by the National Housing Conference, conservatively put the deficit in housing stock at 8.8 million units. Many units are substandard and overcrowded. Massive housing subsidies provided under the income tax code have made it possible for many people to own their own homes, but many others are still excluded or economically pressed to meet housing costs. Forty-eight percent of elderly people and 28 percent of eligible families with children received rental assistance in 1983. New rental housing reached a peak of 530,000 units in the 1970s;

by 1984 the number had shrunk to 94,500.

In 1984, total religious affiliation accounted for 142.2 million people. By major denomination, according to National Council of Churches data, Protestants numbered 78.7 million, Catholics 52.3 million, and Jews 5.8 million; other denominations accounted for the remainder. Between 1979 and 1986, the share of Protestants in the composition of upper-level corporate executives dropped from 68.4 to 58.3 percent; the Catholic share increased from 21.5 to 27.1 percent and the Jewish share, from 5.6 to 7.4 percent.

Voter registration and voting in presidential election years declined between 1968 and 1976; they were higher in 1984 but well below earlier levels. Registration and voting rates are higher among whites than blacks or Hispanics, among women than men (a change from previous years), and among people 45 and over as compared with younger people. Registration and voting are directly correlated with levels of income; they are highest among those with incomes of $50,000 and above and lowest among those with incomes below $5,000. In 1980 and 1984, Democrats outnumbered Republicans and independents. Black registration in 11 southern states rose between 1960 and 1982 from 1.5 to 4.3 million, while white registration increased from 12.3 to 22.9 million. Poll data indicated that the key electoral issues in the late 1970s were inflation and energy; by 1984 these had given way to foreign affairs and unemployment.

We hope that our reports on some facets of societal well-being will encourage others to revive and renew the work of providing useful information on how well our society performs in those aspects of social life that are too often omitted when national leaders and the media provide their appraisals of progress and inventories of unfinished business. In future versions of this volume we hope to offer an enlarged and enriched inventory of social indicators, reflecting the fruits of this labor.

TABLE 6.1. CHARACTERISTICS OF HOUSEHOLDS LIVING IN SUBSIDIZED RENTAL HOUSING, 1980

Subsidized housing provides a significant resource for the poor, especially for female-headed families and older persons living in the central cities.

Characteristics	Percentage	Total Number (in thousands)	Median Income
All households	100.0	2,511	$4,978
Inside metropolitan areas	73.9	1,858	4,959
Inside central cities	54.6	1,373	4,880
Outside central cities	19.3	485	5,386
Outside metropolitan areas	26.0	653	5,078
Northeast	31.6	794	6,172
North Central	21.4	538	4,696
South	32.2	809	4,617
West	14.7	370	4,651
White	58.6	1,473	4,822
Black	38.5	967	5,367
Hispanic origin	8.0	202	6,146
Family households	59.3	1,491	6,812
Married couples	23.7	596	9,507
Male householder	1.1	28	—
Female householder	34.5	867	5,325
Nonfamily households	40.6	1,020	3,955
Male householder	1.1	28	—
Female householder	31.5	792	3,845
Households with member(s) under 19	46.7	1,173	6,475
Householders 65 or over	34.3	863	4,087
Households with member(s) who worked in 1979	39.3	989	8,283
Households with member(s) who did not work in 1979	57.9	1,456	3,981

Sources: U.S. Bureau of the Census, "Characteristics of Households and Persons Receiving Noncash Benefits, 1979," preliminary data from *Current Population Survey*, Table 5 (Washington, D.C.: U.S. Government Printing Office, March 1980); and *Current Population Reports* (Series P-23, No. 110, Washington, D.C.: U.S. Government Printing Office, 1981).

TABLE 6.2 HOUSING STOCK, 1960–1983 (IN THOUSANDS) [a]

Total stock rose by 37 percent between 1970 and 1983; the share representing home ownership was stable over this period, 60 percent in 1983.

Category	1960	1970	1980	1983
Owner-occupied	32,797	39,886	51,795	54,724
Renter-occupied[b]	20,227	23,560	28,595	29,914
Total	56,584	67,699	86,693	91,675

[a]Year-round units.
[b]Includes public or subsidized.
Source: *Statistical Abstract of the United States, 1986,* p. 729.

TABLE 6.3. NEW HOUSING UNITS STARTED, 1960–1984

Housing starts peaked in 1972; they have been below 2 million since 1979.

Year	Total (in thousands)	Publicly Owned (in thousands)
1960	1,296	44
1961	1,365	52
1962	1,492	30
1963	1,635	32
1964	1,561	32
1965	1,510	37
1966	1,196	31
1967	1,322	30
1968	1,545	38
1969	1,500	33
1970	1,469	35
1971	2,085	32
1972	2,379	22
1973	2,057	12
1974	1,353	15
1975	1,171	11
1976	1,548	10
1977	2,002	15
1978	2,036	16
1979	1,760	15
1980	1,313	20
1981	1,100	16
1982	1,072	10
1983	1,712	9
1984	1,756	6

Source: *Statistical Abstract of the United States, 1986,* p. 724.

TABLE 6.4. HOME OWNERSHIP BY RACE, 1960–1983

Two-thirds of whites and less than half of blacks own their own homes.

Race	1960	1970	1980	1983
White	64.4	65.4	67.8	67.7
Black	38.4	41.6	44.4	46.2

Source: *Statistical Abstract of the United States, 1986,* p. 731.

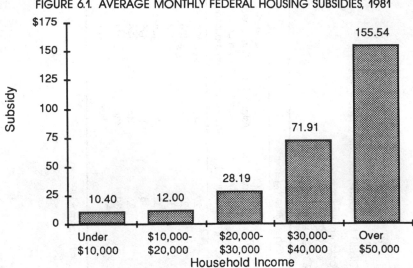

FIGURE 6.1. AVERAGE MONTHLY FEDERAL HOUSING SUBSIDIES, 1981

Source: U.S. House, Committee on Banking, Finance, and Urban Affairs, Subcommittee on Housing and Community Development, *Making Affordable Housing a Reality* (Washington, D.C.: Author, June 1984), p. 189.

TABLE 6.5. ESTIMATES OF HOMELESS IN 40 METROPOLITAN AREAS, WINTER 1984[a,b]

Homelessness became an increasingly important problem in all major metropolitan areas of the United States in the 1980s, on a scale not seen since the depression of the 1930s.

Metropolitan Area	Highest Official Estimate	Metropolitan Area	Highest Official Estimate
Large metropolitan areas		Medium-size metropolitan areas	
Baltimore	750	Baton Rouge, La.	200
Boston	5,000	Birmingham, Ala.	1,000
Chicago	26,000	Charleston, S.C.	250
Cincinnati	1,350	Charlotte, N.C.	400
Cleveland	2,000	Colorado Springs, Colo.	200
Detroit	9,000	Davenport, Iowa	500
Hartford	1,800	Dayton, Ohio	1,000
Houston	12,500	Fort Wayne, Ind.	1,000
Kansas City, Mo.	1,500	Grand Rapids, Mich.	550
Los Angeles	39,000	Little Rock, Ark.	3,000
Miami	10,000	Las Vegas, Nev.	2,000
Minneapolis/St. Paul	1,150	Louisville, Ky.	2,000
New York	50,000	Raleigh, N.C.	225
Philadelphia	8,600	Richmond, Va.	2,250
Phoenix	1,500	Rochester, N.Y.	300
Pittsburgh	1,500	Salt Lake City, Utah	650
Portland	2,700	Scranton, Pa.	100
San Francisco	11,500	Syracuse, N.Y.	450
Seattle	5,000	Tampa, Fla.	1,500
Washington, D.C.	10,500	Worcester, Mass.	3,250

[a]Based on extrapolation of estimates provided by shelter operators, local experts, published estimates, and street and shelter counts.

[b]Advocacy groups have provided evidence that these estimates are far too low; the General Accounting Office casts doubt on both the offical HUD and the advocacy estimates of 2 to 3 million homeless people.

Source: *A Report to the Secretary on Homeless and Emergency Shelters,* p. 14.

TABLE 6.6.   ENROLLMENT IN INSTITUTIONS OF HIGHER EDUCATION, BY SPECIFIED MINORITY GROUPS, 1968–1982

Enrollment rose by two-thirds between 1972 and 1982; among blacks, enrollment rose by 92 percent, and among other minorities it more than doubled. In 1982 total minority enrollment was 17.4 percent of the total, compared with 12.3 percent in 1972.

Year	Number of Institutions	Total Enrollment	Black Enrollment		Other Minority Groups				
			Number (in thousands)	Percentage	Total (in thousands)	Percentage	American Indian (in thousands)	Asian American (in thousands)	Spanish-Surnamed American (in thousands)
1968	2,054	4,820	287	6.0	169	3.5	29	48	91
1970	2,516	4,966	345	6.9	181	3.7	27	52	103
1972	2,665	5,531	459	8.3	219	4.0	32	57	130
1974	2,808	5,639	508	9.0	255	4.5	33	64	158
1976	2,821	5,755	605	10.5	331	5.8	38	101	191
1978	2,897	5,664	601	10.6	346	6.1	36	114	196
1980	2,979	5,993	625	10.4	396	6.6	39	136	221
1982	2,959	5,856	587	10.0	418	7.1	38	156	224

Sources: *Statistical Abstract of the United States, 1982–83,* p. 162; and *Statistical Abstract of the United States, 1986,* p. 153.

TABLE 6.7. PRISONERS UNDER DEATH SENTENCE, 1975–1984

Executions resumed in 1977, after a six-year moratorium. Since World War II, 57 percent of civilian prisoners executed have been black.

Year	Total	White	Black and Other	Black and Other (Percentage)
1975	479	214	265	55.3
1977	423	229	194	45.9
1980	714	427	287	40.2
1981	838	488	350	41.8
1982	1,050	604	446	42.5
1983	1,202	690	512	42.6
1984	1,405	804	585	41.6

Source: *Statistical Abstract of the United States, 1986*, p. 189.

FIGURE 6.2 TOTAL ARRESTS IN THE UNITED STATES AND FEDERAL AND STATE PRISON POPULATIONS, 1972–1984

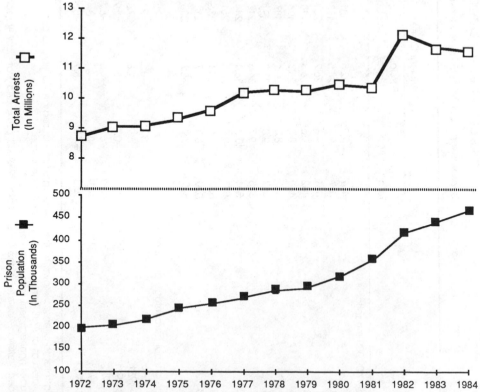

Source: R. L. Bonn, *The Thirteen Year Imprisonment Wave*, paper presented at the Annual Meeting of the Academy of Criminal Justice Sciences (Orlando, Fla., March 1986), pp. 10, 13.

TABLE 6.8. CRIME RATES BY TYPE, 1972–1983[a]

Reported crime rates rose over this period by 34 percent overall; the trends varied by type of crime.

Year	Violent Crime					Property Crime			
	Total	Murder[b]	Forcible Rape	Robbery	Aggravated Assault	Total	Burglary	Larceny Theft	Motor Vehicle Theft
Rate per 100,000 inhabitants									
1972	401	9.0	22.5	181	189	3,560	1,141	1,994	426
1973	417	9.4	24.5	183	201	3,737	1,223	2,072	443
1974	461	9.8	26.2	209	216	4,389	1,438	2,490	462
1975	482	9.6	26.3	218	227	4,800	1,526	2,805	469
1976	460	8.8	26.4	196	229	4,807	1,439	2,921	446
1977	467	8.8	29.1	187	242	4,588	1,411	2,730	448
1978	487	9.0	30.8	191	256	4,622	1,424	2,744	455
1979	535	9.7	34.5	212	279	4,986	1,499	2,988	499
1980	581	10.2	36.4	244	291	5,319	1,668	3,156	495
1981	577	9.8	35.6	251	281	5,223	1,632	3,122	469
1982	562	9.1	34.1	236	283	5,024	1,485	3,082	457
1983	529	8.3	33.7	214	273	4,630	1,334	2,866	429
1984	539	7.9	35.7	205	290	4,492	1,264	2,791	437
Average annual percentage of change									
1972–1976	8.2	3.7	−0.5	2.1	5.3	8.8	6.5	11.6	1.2
1977–1981	3.7	5.9	2.8	7.6	4.1	3.5	3.9	3.6	1.2
1980–1981	−1.7	−0.7	−3.9	2.9	−3.3	−1.8	−2.2	−1.1	−5.2
1981–1982	−2.9	−6.7	−4.5	−6.7	0.8	−3.4	−8.8	−0.7	−2.6
1982–1983	−4.9	−8.1	—	−8.4	−2.4	−6.9	−9.2	−6.0	−5.1
1983–1984	0.3	−4.8	5.9	−5.1	3.9	−3.1	−5.5	−2.7	1.5

[a]Data refer to offenses known to the police; rates are based on U.S. Bureau of the Census estimated resident population as of July 1, except 1980, enumerated as of April 1; minus sign (−) denotes decrease.
[b]Includes nonnegligent manslaughter.
Sources: *Statistical Abstract of the United States 1982–83*, p.174; and *Statistical Abstract of the United States, 1986*, p. 166.

TABLE 6.9. PERCENTAGE OF HIGH SCHOOL SENIORS WHO USED DRUGS IN LAST 12 MONTHS, 1975–1984[a]

Most indicators declined from the peak levels in the 1978–1980 period.

Type of Drugs[b]	Class									
	1975 (n=9,400)	1976 (n=15,400)	1977 (n=17,100)	1978 (n=17,800)	1979 (n=15,500)	1980 (n=15,900)	1981 (n=17,500)	1982 (n=17,700)	1983 (n=16,300)	1984 (n=15,900)
Marijuana, hashish	40.0	44.5	47.6	50.2	50.8	48.8	46.1	44.3	42.3	40.0
Hallucinogens	11.2	9.4	8.8	9.6	9.9	9.3	9.0	8.1	7.3	6.5
Cocaine	5.6	6.0	7.2	9.0	12.0	12.3	12.4	11.5	11.4	11.6
Stimulants	16.2	15.8	16.3	17.1	18.3	20.8	26.0	26.1	24.6	—
Sedatives	11.7	10.7	10.8	9.9	9.9	10.3	10.5	9.1	7.9	6.6
Alcohol	84.8	85.7	87.0	87.7	88.1	87.9	87.0	86.8	87.3	86.0

[a]Data collected in annual surveys of high school seniors conducted by NIDA.
[b]Excludes use of prescribed medications.
Source: National Institute on Drug Abuse, Research Analysis and Utilization System: *Preventive Research, 1985* (Rockville, Md.: Monograph Series No. 63, 1985), p. 4.

TABLE 6.10. VOTING AND REGISTRATION, PRESIDENTIAL ELECTIONS, 1968 AND 1984 (PERCENTAGE)

Voting participation was lower in 1984 than in 1968 among all groups and in all areas. Only among blacks was registration higher in 1984.

	1968[a]		1984[b]	
	Registered	Voted	Registered	Voted
Percentage of total	74.3	67.8	68.3	59.9
White	74.3	69.1	69.6	61.4
Black	66.2	57.6	66.3	55.8
Spanish origin	—	—	40.1	32.6
Male	76.0	69.8	67.3	59.0
Female	72.8	66.0	69.3	60.8
North and West				
Percentage of total				
in North and West	76.5	71.0	69.0	61.6
White	77.2	71.8	70.5	63.0
Black	71.8	64.8	67.2	58.9
South				
Percentage of total				
in South	69.2	60.1	66.9	56.8
White	70.8	61.9	67.8	58.1
Black	61.6	59.6	65.6	53.2

[a]Total number of voting age, 116,535,000.
[b]Total number of voting age, 169,963,000.
Source: U.S. Bureau of the Census, "Voting and Registration in the Election of November 1984," in *Current Population Reports* (Series P-20, No. 397, Washington, D.C.: U.S. Government Printing Office, January 1985), pp. 1, 3.

FIGURE 6.3. VOTER PARTICIPATION IN PRESIDENTIAL ELECTIONS, 1964–1984 (PERCENTAGE)

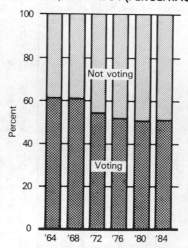

Source: *Statistical Abstract of the United States, 1986,* p. xxiii.

SECTION 7. HEALTH STATUS AND MEDICAL CARE

The pace and scope of change in health care in the 1980s was as great as at any time since the enactment of Medicare and Medicaid in 1965. Concern about costs of care came to dominate public policy. Investor-owned providers became major factors in an industry previously dominated by community-based hospitals, physicians, and nonprofit third-party payers. The public share of health care spending stabilized and fell slightly in the 1980s after increasing in the two previous decades. Physicians increasingly worked in group practices (three or more) or other organized settings (clinics, hospitals, and so on). In 1984, an estimated 40 percent were in some form of group practice; half of patient-physician encounters occur in organized settings.

Although health indicators showed continuing improvement, racial disparities persist. Medicaid has improved the care and health of those who qualify; about half of all poor people, including 5 million children and six of every ten women of childbearing age with incomes below the poverty line, remained ineligible. Hospital occupancy rates and average lengths of stay declined; in 1985 the occupancy rate was below 70 percent in more than two-thirds of hospitals and below 60 percent in half of them.

The *Fortune* list of the 500 largest nonfinancial corporations for 1985 included four investor-owned medical care providers: Hospital Corporation of America (number 11), National Medical Enterprises (number 24), American Medical International (number 31), and Humana (number 33). Investor-owned corporations are also active in developing HMOs (health maintenance organizations). HMO enrollments more than doubled between 1975 and 1980 and doubled again between 1980 and 1985 to reach a total of about 11 million—one-fourth of them in the largest HMO, Kaiser-Permanente. By 1984, seven of the fourteen largest HMOs were investor-owned and were enrolling about half of all new members. Investor-owned PPOs (preferred provider organizations) also grew quickly. Stock prices of major investor-owned HMOs rose by two to five times or more between 1983 and April 1985. Investor-owned corporations are involved in direct ownership, joint ventures with nonprofit agencies, management contracts, and in other ways. In the mid-1980s, they were actively diversifying into activities that combined higher profit potential with less regulation—for example, psychiatric care, long-term care, drug treatment centers, and rehabilitation centers. They are also active in nursing homes and favor areas like the Southwest and the South, where regulatory burdens are lightest. Recent studies indicate that investor-owned hospitals represent 13 percent of the nationwide total, as high as 30 to 44 percent in Florida, Texas, Tennessee, and Virginia. The 10 largest investor-owned firms owned or managed 11 percent of total hospital beds in 1983. By one estimate, investor-owned providers received 20 to 25 percent of all payments for personal health care in 1985.

The number of nursing home residents rose by 18 percent between 1965 and 1970, 17 percent between 1970 and 1975, 14 percent between 1975 and 1980, and an estimated 12 percent between 1980 and 1985. The number and share of the population in nursing homes is expected to decline in the future. Four of every five nursing homes are for-profit.

During a typical recent year, 18.5 million people had no health care coverage throughout the year and 16 million lacked coverage for five months or more—a total of 12 percent of the population. Most are young, black, or Hispanic, with low income. Coverage is high among the Medicare population, but the program covers only 75 percent of hospital costs and 58 percent of physicians' costs. Participants paid out of pocket for 11 percent of hospital costs and 26 percent of physicians' costs. The Medicare hospital deductible was $400 in 1984, compared with $180 in 1980. Fifty-one percent of nursing home costs are paid out of pocket. The Part B premium for Medicare in 1986 was $15.50 per month; it was $9.60 in 1980 and $8.20 in 1978. Significant numbers of physicians limit or refrain entirely from participation in Medicare and Medicaid. About 81 million people had some form of dental insurance in 1984. Eighty-four percent of costs for eye care are out of pocket; the total for 1984 was $1.6 billion.

A 1986 study estimated that in 1983 administrative costs accounted for $77 billion, or 22 percent of total health care expenditures. This compares with 6 percent in the United Kingdom and 8 percent in Canada; a decentralized, mixed, private-public system is costly to operate.

In the 1980s, major employers had begun large-scale efforts to control costs through direct intervention and participation in health care decisions, reimbursement, and forms of treatment, as well as through cost-sharing by employees. Contracts with HMOs, PPOs, and hospitals setting negotiated rates and providing for access to cost data were part of this effort. Other measures include workplace wellness, antismoking, diet, and exercise programs; monitoring of high utilization by both patients and physicians; efforts to manage stress at work; increased attention by physicians to prevention of illness and health maintenance; mandatory second opinions and precertifications for nonemergency surgery; preference for ambulatory diagnosis and treatment over hospital admissions; preemployment health screening; and a range of other strategies.

Studies indicate that psychotropic drugs are dispensed or prescribed in about 10 percent of all visits to physicians' offices; four-fifths were antianxiety and antidepressant drugs. Between 1972 and 1981, surgery rates for people 65 and over rose by 106 percent, compared with a 49 percent increase for all people; surgical mortality rates in this period declined 12 percent for patients 75 and over and 6 percent for those age 65 to 74.

A majority of users of home health care services are under 65, but those over 65 use the most home care services. Persons with chronic conditions constitute 10 percent of the population and account for 30 percent of health care expenditures. An estimated 2.7 million people were unable to work because of long-term health problems, and 5.4 million had problems that limited their activities. The incidence of limited activity because of chronic health problems is higher among low-income than other people. Estimated loss of earnings of people unable to work was $28.1 billion, lost workday earnings were $11 billion, and disability costs were $12.7 billion, for a total of $51.9 billion in 1975; these numbers correlate with declines in labor force participation by men between 1969 and 1980. The most important causes of involun-

tary withdrawal from work were orthopedic impairments, chronic heart disease, respiratory illness, arthritis, disk displacement, and job-related injuries. An estimated 11 million people who lost their jobs for all reasons in 1982 also lost health care coverage.

After the cuts in funding for health planning in 1981 and subsequent years, capital outlays by health care providers rose from $4 billion in 1979 to $11 billion in 1982. Between 1979 and 1982, the number of CAT scans increased from 194,000 to 600,000. There were 1,716 scanners in use in 1982. In 1983, the Food and Drug Administration reported a risk of excessive radiation involving 238 scanners.

Between 1981 and 1985 the number of kidney transplants rose from 4,885 to 7,800, heart transplants from 62 to 719, and liver transplants from 26 to 602. Estimated initial costs range from $35,000 for a kidney transplant to $130,000 for a liver transplant.

Over a characteristic three-year period, more than one family in four not on Medicare or Medicaid will spend $3,000 or more to meet the costs of a major illness. Fewer than half of all families are protected against the cost of catastrophic illness.

In 1984–1985, about 800 different measures were adopted in all 50 states to control increases in Medicaid costs. They included freezing physician fees and hospital reimbursement rates, imposing copayments and deductibles, requiring preadmission screening, requiring second opinions for elective surgery, and limiting capital spending.

In the late 1970s and early 1980s, as the number of physicians increased more rapidly than did traditional urban opportunities to practice, small towns and communities were able to attract increasing numbers of physicians. Another sign of increased numbers of physicians was the tripling of walk-in medical care centers between 1983 and 1985.

In 1984, the medical licensing boards of the states and the District of Columbia revoked a total of 255 licenses to practice medicine, or one for every 1,701 practicing physicians. Other disciplinary action was taken against one of every 318 physicians, varying widely by states. Twenty states require physicians to attend continuing medical education courses as a condition of licensure;

25 states have comparable requirements for social workers.

Low birthweight has declined in all regions except one. The black rate was about double the white rate in all regions and among all age groups of mothers. More black and Hispanic mothers of low-birthweight infants do not receive prenatal care. In 1970, the death rate per 100,000 abortions exceeded the infant mortality rate. *Roe* v. *Wade,* the Supreme Court case resulting in legalization of abortions, was decided in 1973. In 1972, the infant mortality rate was 3.7 times the abortion death rate, and in 1980 it was 15 times as high.

The Centers for Disease Control projected 14,700 AIDS cases for 1986; the number is expected to continue to increase unless effective countermeasures are developed.

The level of public concern with the state of health of our health care system reached new heights in the early 1980s, mirroring the perceptions of many that it increasingly costs more and delivers less than in the past. How these concerns will be reflected by changed policies in the future cannot be predicted, but one can project a health care system quite different in key respects from the present one. A serious, well-informed society can move toward a system that costs less, provides better care, achieves a better balance between curing illness and sustaining health, and treats all who use it equally and compassionately.

TABLE 7.1. HEALTH CARE EXPENDITURES IN DOLLARS PER CAPITA AND AS PERCENTAGE OF GROSS NATIONAL PRODUCT (GNP), 1950–1984

Total expenditures increased by 56 percent between 1980 and 1984. Inflation raised the per capita cost more rapidly than the share of GNP; both grew without interruption in this period. Per capita costs rose 51 percent between 1980 and 1984. The public share has exceeded 40 percent of the total since 1974, declined after 1984.

| Year | Dollars Per Capita | | | | Public Expenditures as Percentage of Total |
	All Health Care Expenditures (in billions)	Personal Health Care	All Health Care	Percentage of GNP	
1950	$12.7	70	82	4.4	27.2
1960	26.9	129	145	5.3	24.7
1970	75.0	305	350	7.6	37.0
1980	248.0	958	1,049	9.4	42.7
1984	387.4	—	1,580	10.6	41.4

Sources: U.S. Public Health Service, *Health—United States, 1984* (Washington, D.C.: U.S. Government Printing Office, 1985), pp. 132, 137, 146; and *Health—United States, 1985*, pp. 128, 130.

TABLE 7.2 SOURCES OF PAYMENT FOR PERSONAL HEALTH CARE, 1960–1984 (PERCENTAGE)

Government pays the largest share of costs. Direct payments fell but remain about 25 percent of all costs.

| Year | Third Party | | Government | Direct Payment |
	Private Health Insurance	Philanthropy and Industry		
1960	21.1	2.3	21.8	54.9
1970	23.4	1.7	34.3	40.5
1980	30.7	1.2	39.6	28.5
1984	31.3	1.2	39.6	27.9

Source: *Health—United States, 1985*, p. 136.

TABLE 7.3. ENROLLMENTS IN MEDICARE PARTS A (HOSPITAL INSURANCE) AND B (SUPPLEMENTARY MEDICAL INSURANCE) (IN THOUSANDS), 1970–1983

Women enrollees substantially outnumber men; most Medicare enrollees find it necessary to purchase Part B coverage.

| Year | Hospital Insurance | | | Supplementary Medical Insurance | | |
	Men	Women	Total	Men	Women	Total
1970	8,507	11,855	20,361	8,132	11,452	19,584
1975	9,168	13,304	22,472	8,873	13,073	21,945
1980	10,156	14,948	25,104	9,868	14,813	24,680
1983	10,755	15,915	26,670	10,479	15,813	26,292

Source: *Social Security Bulletin, Annual Statistical Supplement, 1984–85*, p. 206.

FIGURE 7.1. U.S. HEALTH CARE PAYMENTS AND EXPENDITURES, 1984

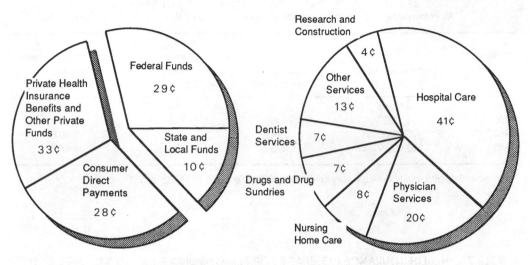

Sources of Payment, Personal Health Care

Types of Expenditures

Source: *Health—United States, 1985,* pp. 146–147.

TABLE 7.4. MEDICAID RECIPIENTS BY CATEGORY, 1972–1984 (IN THOUSANDS)

Enrollment peaked in 1977 and then fell; disbursements continued to increase steadily. AFDC recipients constitute 72 percent of all Medicaid recipients.

Year	Total[a]	Aged 65 or Older	Blindness	Total Disability	Families with Dependent Children[a] Adults	Children	Other
Ending June							
1972	17,606	3,318	108	1,625	3,137	7,841	1,576
1975	22,013	3,643	106	2,265	4,529	9,598	1,800
Ending September							
1977	22,831	3,636	92	2,710	4,785	9,651	1,959
1980	21,605	3,440	92	2,819	4,877	9,333	1,499
1981	21,980	3,367	86	2,993	5,187	9,581	1,364
1982	21,603	3,240	84	2,806	5,356	9,563	1,434
1983	21,554	3,371	77	2,844	5,592	9,535	1,129
1984	21,365	3,165	80	2,870	5,598	9,771	1,185

[a]Beginning in FY1980, recipients' categories do not add to unduplicated total because of the small number of recipients that are in more than one category during the year. Includes small number of recipients eligible due to blindness.

Source: *Social Security Bulletin, Annual Statistical Supplement, 1984–85,* pp. 219, 221–222.

TABLE 7.5. HOSPITAL CHARGES UNDER MEDICARE, 1970–1983

Reimbursements rose rapidly; rising daily charges were somewhat offset by declines in length of stay and in the share of total charges covered by Medicare. Reimbursements covered a smaller share of total costs than in previous years.

Year	Reimbursements (in millions)	Charges per Day (in dollars)	Average Number of Days Covered	Reimbursements as Percentage of Total Charges
1970	4,500.8	76	12.4	77.2
1975	9,835.7	145	10.6	75.1
1980	22,013.6	294	9.9	69.6
1983	33,509.9	478	9.1	64.9

Source: *Social Security Bulletin, Annual Statistical Supplement, 1984–85*, p. 209.

TABLE 7.6. HEALTH INSURANCE COVERAGE FOR PERSONS UNDER 65 YEARS OF AGE, BY TYPE OF COVERAGE AND SELECTED CHARACTERISTICS, 1978, 1980, AND 1982[a]

The share of uninsured persons rose, most rapidly after 1980. Fewer blacks had private coverage, more were Medicaid clients; total coverage for blacks was below that of whites. Thirty-seven percent of people in the lowest income group and 28 percent in the next to lowest had no coverage. Coverage was lower in the South and West than in the North.

Category	Private Insurance[b] (percentage)			Medicaid[b] (percentage)			Not Covered (percentage)		
	1978	1980	1982	1978	1980	1982	1978	1980	1982
Total	78.7	78.8	77.3	6.1	5.9	5.6	12.2	12.4	14.7
Race									
White	81.8	81.9	80.4	4.0	3.9	3.6	11.1	11.4	13.5
Black	59.2	60.1	59.6	19.7	17.9	17.2	18.7	19.0	21.2
Family Income[c]									
Less than $7,000	42.3	38.6	38.3	26.0	27.6	24.9	29.5	31.0	35.0
$7,000–$9,999	65.4	61.1	67.6	7.2	9.2	4.4	22.6	25.9	24.7
$10,000–$14,999	82.9	79.0	81.3	2.4	3.0	2.0	11.2	15.0	14.2
$15,000–$24,999	91.8	90.2	91.8	0.9	1.1	0.7	4.7	6.2	5.7
$25,000 or more	94.3	93.7	93.8	0.4	0.6	0.5	3.6	3.9	4.1
Geographic Region									
Northeast	81.5	81.7	80.5	7.3	7.0	6.9	10.0	10.3	11.0
North Central	85.0	83.8	82.0	5.5	5.8	5.8	8.0	9.0	10.9
South	73.9	75.6	74.3	5.6	4.8	4.6	15.6	15.0	17.5
West	74.6	74.3	72.4	6.4	6.5	5.8	15.0	15.3	19.1

[a]Survey data.
[b]Persons with both private insurance and Medicaid appear in both columns.
[c]Family income categories for 1978 and 1980; income categories in 1982 are less than $10,000, $10,000–$14,999, $15,000–$19,999, $20,000–$34,999, $35,000 or more.
Source: *Health—United States, 1985*, p. 146.

TABLE 7.7. ADMISSIONS AND OUTPATIENT VISITS IN SHORT-STAY HOSPITALS BY TYPE OF OWNERSHIP, UNITED STATES, SELECTED YEARS, 1970–1983[a] (IN THOUSANDS)

Total hospital admissions were relatively stable after 1980, but rose substantially between 1970 and 1980. Outpatient visits rose until 1982, then fell for all hospitals. Admissions to proprietary hospitals rose most (63 percent) over the 1970–1982 period; admissions to public hospitals rose least (15 percent).

Category	1970	1980	1981	1982	1983
Admissions					
All ownerships	30,706	38,140	38,417	38,332	38,135
Federal	1,454	1,942	1,923	1,903	1,934
Nonfederal	29,252	36,198	36,494	36,429	36,201
Nonprofit	20,948	25,576	25,955	25,908	25,837
Proprietary	2,031	3,165	3,239	3,316	3,299
State and local government	6,273	7,458	7,299	7,205	7,064
Outpatient visits[b]					
All ownerships	173,058	255,320	257,254	304,089	263,729
Federal	39,514	48,568	50,524	53,200	49,734
Nonfederal	133,545	206,752	206,729	250,888	213,995
Nonprofit	90,992	142,864	143,953	176,838	151,444
Proprietary	4,698	9,696	9,961	13,193	10,389
State and local government	37,854	54,192	52,816	60,857	52,163

[a]Data based on reporting by a census of registered hospitals, excluding psychiatric and tuberculosis and other respiratory disease hospitals.
[b]Because of modifications in the collection of outpatient data for 1982, there are discontinuities in the trends for this item.
Source: *Health—United States, 1985,* p. 87.

TABLE 7.8. PHYSICIANS PER 100,000 POPULATION BY REGION, 1970, 1980, AND 1983

All regions showed an increase in the physician-population ratio; the Northeast and the West maintained higher ratios than the North Central and South regions.

Region	1970	1980	1983
Northeast	185.0	224.8	242.9
North Central	127.5	165.8	177.7
South	114.8	157.1	165.0
West	158.2	200.1	205.2
United States total	142.4	182.4	192.6

Source: *Health—United States, 1985,* p. 109.

TABLE 7.9. CREDENTIALS OF MEDICAID PARTICIPANTS, 1980 (PERCENTAGE)

Older physicians, those without board certification, and foreign medical graduates were more prevalent in the large Medicaid practices than among all physicians who treated Medicaid patients.

Primary Care Physicians	All Medicaid Participants	LMP[a] Physicians
General practitioners	39.9	39.8
Board certified	39.5	26.4
Foreign medical graduates	13.8	20.1
Sixty years or older	30.4	36.7
No hospital affiliation	1.8	2.9

[a]Large Medicaid practices (LMP) have at least 30 percent Medicaid patients; these practices are a subset of all Medicaid participants.
Source: "Access to Private Physicians for Public Patients: Participation in Medicaid and Medicare," p. 107.

TABLE 7.10. SELECTED RATES OF NONFEDERAL SHORT-STAY HOSPITAL UTILIZATION AND BENEFIT PAYMENTS FOR MEDICARE ENROLLEES 65 YEARS OF AGE AND OVER, BY GEOGRAPHIC DIVISION, 1978, 1980, AND 1983[a]

Lengths of stay fell in all areas, remaining highest in the Northeast. Charges rose in all areas as did benefit payments. The share of costs reimbursed by Medicare was in the 68–70 percent range over this period.

Geographic Division	Average Number of Days in Short-Stay Hospitals			Average Covered Per-Day Charges in Short-Stay Hospitals[b]			Benefit Payments Per Enrollee					
							Hospital Insurance[c]			Supplementary Medical Insurance		
	1978	1980	1983	1978	1980	1983	1978	1980	1983[d]	1978	1980	1983[d]
United States	10.8	10.7	9.8	$226	$296	$448	$664	$893	$1,324	$261	$363	$589
New England	12.1	12.2	10.9	236	300	459	760	966	1,399	266	376	618
Middle Atlantic	13.8	13.6	12.6	243	308	463	722	949	1,402	296	400	668
East North Central	11.5	11.3	10.3	233	296	490	734	983	1,433	233	341	550
West North Central	10.4	10.3	9.1	188	250	434	646	872	1,300	203	288	443
South Atlantic	10.4	10.3	9.5	211	276	467	592	802	1,213	264	359	584
East South Central	9.9	9.6	8.8	181	244	415	513	747	1,156	184	259	418
West South Central	9.3	9.1	8.5	191	255	441	572	790	1,245	236	326	532
Mountain	8.9	8.8	8.0	230	309	543	560	767	1,106	258	343	577
Pacific	8.8	8.8	7.9	317	424	731	721	980	1,418	346	471	758

[a]Data compiled by Health Care Financing Administration.
[b]Includes reimbursable charges and days of care covered by Medicare.
[c]Short-stay hospitals accounted for approximately 93 percent of all hospital insurance reimbursements.
[d]Estimated.
Source: *Health—United States, 1985*, p. 149.

TABLE 7.11. SOURCE OF PHYSICIAN CARE BY RACE AND INCOME, 1983 (PERCENTAGE)[a]

Blacks and low-income people of all races rely on emergency rooms and outpatient clinics more and use doctors' offices and the telephone less.

Category	Doctor's Office	Emergency Room	Hospital Outpatient Clinic or Telephone
All	55.9	14.9	15.5
White	57.4	13.4	16.2
Black	44.1	26.5	9.7
Income Level			
Less than $10,000	49.8	18.4	12.3
$10,000–$14,999	52.2	17.7	13.2
$15,000–$19,999	54.2	16.7	16.3
$20,000–$34,999	59.0	13.2	16.2
$35,000 or more	59.6	11.5	18.8

[a]Includes source or place unknown.
Source: *Health—United States, 1985,* p. 82.

TABLE 7.12. AVERAGE OF INDIVIDUALS' VISITS TO PHYSICIANS PER YEAR BY RACE AND INCOME, 1964, 1980, AND 1983 (NUMBER PER PERSON)

Differences of access by race and income narrowed substantially, and access by the poor greatly increased after the introduction of Medicaid and Medicare.

Category	1964	1980	1983
White	4.7	4.8	5.1
Black	3.6	4.6	4.8
Income level			
Less than $7,000	3.9	5.5	5.9[a]
$7,000–$9,999	4.2	4.4	5.0
$10,000–$14,000	4.7	4.9	4.7[b]
$15,000–$24,999	4.8	4.7	5.0[c]
$25,000 or more	5.2	4.6	5.4[d]

[a]Less than $10,000.
[b]$15,000–$19,999.
[c]$20,000–$34,999.
[d]$34,000 or more.
Sources: *Health—United States, 1982,* p. 90; and *Health—United States, 1985,* p. 82.

TABLE 7.13. EMPLOYMENT IN HEALTH CARE, 1970, 1980, AND 1984

Substantial growth occurred over this period, with more employed in hospitals than in all other categories combined.

Category	1970	1980	1984
	(in thousands)		
Physicians and others in physicians' office	477	777	896
Dentists' office	222	415	468
Hospitals	2,690	4,036	4,228
Convalescent institutions	509	1,199	1,362
Other	349	912	854
Total	4,245	7,339	7,934

Source: *Health—United States, 1985,* p. 105.

TABLE 7.14. TOTAL ENROLLMENT OF MINORITIES AND WOMEN IN SCHOOLS FOR SELECTED HEALTH OCCUPATIONS, UNITED STATES, ACADEMIC YEARS 1971–1972 AND 1983–1984

Women's share of places in health-related professional schools rose substantially except in nursing schools, which have always been predominantly female. Black and other minority enrollments rose modestly and remained relatively low in 1983–1984.

| | Enrollment | | Percentage[a] | | | | | | | |
| | | | Black | | Other Minority | | Women | | | |
Health Occupation	1971–1972	1983–1984	1971–1972	1983–1984	1971–1972	1983–1984	1971–1972	1983–1984
Allopathic	43,650	67,327	4.7	5.5	2.4	9.5	10.9	30.6
Osteopathic	2,304	5,822[b]	1.2	2.0[b]	1.6	4.1[b]	3.4	22.6[b]
Podiatry	1,268	2,556	2.1	6.6	1.1	5.0	1.2	18.6
Dentistry	17,305	21,428	3.5	4.7	2.8	9.4	1.4	22.1
Optometry	3,094	4,561[b]	1.0	1.3[b]	4.9	8.5[b]	3.6	24.6[b]
Pharmacy	16,808	18,831	3.8	5.1	6.2	6.2	24.0	52.2
Veterinary medicine	5,149	8,672	1.8	2.3	0.7	2.9	11.5	47.1
Registered nurses	213,127	234,864[c]	7.3	6.6[c]	2.5	4.0[c]	95.4	95.3[c]
Public health	—	7,614[b]	—	5.8[b]	—	11.4[b]	—	60.7[b]

[a]Percentages based only on total counts of students identified by race/ethnicity and gender.
[b]Data are for 1982–1983.
[c]Data are for 1980–1982.
Source: *Health—United States, 1985,* p. 112.

TABLE 7.15. GRADUATES OF HEALTH PROFESSIONAL SCHOOLS ACCORDING TO PROFESSION, UNITED STATES, SELECTED ESTIMATES AND PROJECTIONS, 1950–2000

The number of medical school graduates declined for the first time in 1983, remaining above levels of the 1970s. Nursing school graduates in the 1980s—slightly below the peak levels of 1978—were expected to decline substantially.

Year	Medicine	Osteopathy	Nursing	Dentistry
1950	5,553	373	25,790	2,565
1960	7,081	427	29,895	3,253
1970	8,367	432	43,103	3,749
1975	12,714	702	73,915	4,969
1978	14,393	963	77,874	5,324
1979	14,966	1,004	77,132	5,424
1980	15,135	1,059	75,523	5,256
1981	15,667	1,151	73,985	5,550
1982	15,985	1,017	74,052	5,371
1983	15,824	1,317	77,408	5,756
1990[a]	16,240	1,480	68,400	4,390
2000[a]	16,080	1,460	57,800	4,080

[a]Projected.
Source: *Health—United States, 1985*, p. 111.

TABLE 7.16. PERCENTAGE DISTRIBUTION OF SELECTED HEALTH PROFESSIONALS BY RACE OR ETHNICITY, 1980[a]

Except for Asians, minorities were significantly underrepresented in these occupations.

Category	White	Black	Hispanic	Asian	American Indian
Physicians	83.0	3.0	4.0	10.0	0.1
Dentists	92.0	2.0	2.0	3.0	0.2
Pharmacists	90.0	3.0	2.0	5.0	0.1
Total population	80.0	12.0	8.0	2.0	0.5

[a]Because of rounding, totals do not add to 100 percent.
Source: *U.S. Public Health Service, Public Health Report* (Washington, D.C.: U.S. Government Printing Office, November–December 1985), p. 677.

TABLE 7.17.   AGE-ADJUSTED DEATH RATES[a] BY SELECTED CAUSE, RACE, AND SEX, UNITED STATES, 1983

The risk of death from all causes shown is higher for blacks than for whites, except for suicide. Homicide is the most dramatic example. Among medical causes of death, diabetes poses the highest relative risk to blacks.

Cause of Death	Black Male	White Male	Relative Risk[b]	Black Female	White Female	Relative Risk[b]
Total deaths	1,019.6	698.4	1.5	590.4	392.7	1.5
Heart disease	308.2	257.8	1.2	191.5	126.7	1.5
Stroke	64.2	35.2	1.8	53.8	29.6	1.8
Cancer	232.2	158.9	1.5	129.8	108.5	1.2
Suicide	10.5	19.3	0.5	2.1	5.6	0.4
Homicide	53.8	8.4	6.4	11.2	2.8	4.0
Accident	66.2	51.8	1.3	21.9	18.3	1.2
Cirrhosis	22.8	13.4	1.7	10.8	6.0	1.8
Diabetes	17.7	9.2	1.9	21.1	8.6	2.5

[a]Rate per 100,000 population.
[b]Black to white.
Source: *Health—United States, 1985,* pp. 46–47.

TABLE 7.18.   LIFE EXPECTANCY AT BIRTH BY RACE AND SEX, UNITED STATES, SELECTED YEARS, 1900–1984

Life expectancy rose for all groups. Female-male and white-black differences remained significant; life expectancies for blacks in 1984 reached levels that applied to whites many years earlier.

Year	All Races Male	All Races Female	White Male	White Female	Black Male	Black Female
1900	46.3	48.3	46.6	48.7	32.5	33.5
1950	65.6	71.1	66.5	72.2	58.9	62.7
1970	67.1	74.8	68.0	75.6	60.0	68.3
1980	70.0	77.4	70.7	78.1	63.8	72.5
1984	71.1	78.3	71.8	78.8	65.5	73.7

Source: *Health—United States, 1985,* p. 40.

TABLE 7.19. INFANT MORTALITY RATES BY RACE, SELECTED YEARS 1950–1983[a]

Infant mortality rates fell to new lows. Racial differences are significant and persistent; the rate for blacks in 1983 had been achieved for whites in the 1960s.

Year	Total	White	Black
1950	29.2	26.8	43.9
1960	26.0	22.9	44.3
1970	20.0	17.8	32.6
1980	12.6	11.0	21.4
1983	11.2	9.7	19.2

[a]Deaths of infants under one year of age per 1,000 live births.
Source: *Health—United States, 1985,* p. 41.

FIGURE 7.2 INFANTS WEIGHING LESS THAN 2,500 GRAMS AT BIRTH, BY RACE AND ETHNICITY OF MOTHER, UNITED STATES, 1983 (PERCENTAGE)[a]

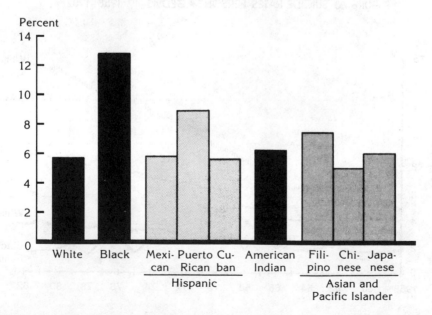

[a]Data are available on race of mother from all states, but data on Hispanic origin of mother are available from only 23 states. However, approximately 90 percent of all births to Hispanic mothers take place among residents of those 23 states.

Source: *Health—United States, 1985.*

TABLE 7.20. HOMICIDE AND SUICIDE RATES FOR MALES AGED 15–34, BY RACE, 1950–1983 (PER 100,000)

Young white males are more likely to commit suicide than blacks in the same age cohort; young black males, however, are much more likely to be murdered than are their white counterparts. There appears to be an upward trend in both suicides and homicides among white youths; trends for blacks' untimely deaths are less well defined.

| | Homicide Victim Rate | | | | Suicide Rate | | | |
| | White | | Black | | White | | Black | |
Year	15–24	25–34	15–24	25–34	15–24	25–34	15–24	25–34
1950	3.7	5.4	58.9	110.5	6.6	13.8	4.9	9.3
1960	4.4	6.2	46.4	92.0	8.6	14.9	4.1	12.4
1970	7.9	13.0	102.5	158.5	13.9	19.9	10.5	19.2
1980	15.5	10.9	84.3	145.1	21.4	25.6	12.3	21.8
1983	11.5	14.9	66.8	102.0	20.6	26.2	11.5	19.1

Source: *Mental Health United States, 1985*, pp. 60, 62.

FIGURE 7.3. SUICIDE RATES, PERSONS AGED 15–19, 1958–1982

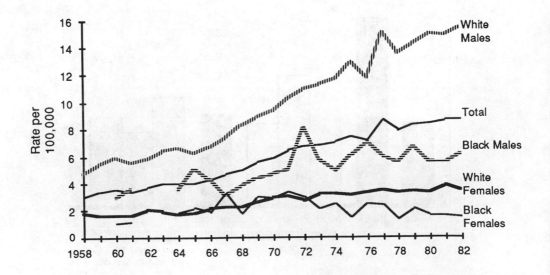

Source: Data from U.S. National Institute of Mental Health, *Mental Health United States, 1985* (Washington, D.C.: Author, 1985), pp. 150–154.

TABLE 7.21. AIDS IN THE UNITED STATES, 1981–1985

The number of AIDS cases rose by 109 percent between 1983 and 1984 and 89 percent between 1984 and 1985.

Year	Cases Diagnosed					
	Bisexual and Homosexual Men	Intravenous Drug Users and Homosexual Men	Intravenous Drug Users Only	All Other Adults	Pediatric Cases	All Cases
1981	178	16	22	11	0	227
1982	473	66	138	99	16	792
1983	1,341	211	392	217	35	2,196
1984	2,939	418	785	397	48	4,582
1985	5,669	599	1,429	840	132	8,661
Percentage of cases in 1985	65.5	6.9	16.5	9.6	1.5	100

Source: U.S. Public Health Service, Centers for Disease Control, *Morbidity and Mortality Weekly Report* (Atlanta, Ga.: Author, January 17, 1986), p. 35.

FIGURE 7.4. AIDS CASES AND DEATHS, 1981–1986, WITH PROJECTIONS TO 1991

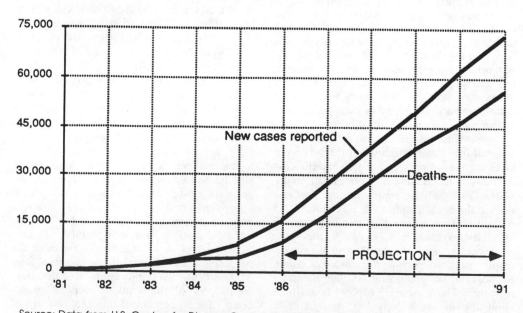

Source: Data from U.S. Centers for Disease Control (Atlanta, Ga., 1986).

SECTION 8. MENTAL HEALTH AND ILLNESS

The information in this section focuses on problems of mental illness. The provision of in- and outpatient care involves many hospitals, clinics, community mental health centers, day centers, social service organizations, and a large group of practitioners engaged in private practice. The focus on the phenomenon of mental illness may obscure the fact that the vast majority of Americans believe that they are relatively free of mental impairment and do not seek professional assistance of any kind. It is much easier to provide information about mental illness in the population than to characterize mental health in positive terms. Preventive services, which seek to avert the onset of severe mental disturbances and to maintain the general level of mental health in the population, are growing. A burgeoning hospice movement is providing care for the dying and their families; many hospices include "respite" programs for caregivers. Using the skills of social workers, whose clients include both workers and their families, employee assistance programs have been developed at various worksites. Research by universities and pharmaceutical companies has expanded and refined the knowledge base regarding dopamine; neurobiological processes; the effects of diet, exercise, and meditation; cultural differences; and the diagnoses and treatments for mental disorder. Self-help human-potential groups are influencing and assisting the general public in perceiving mental health as existing along a continuum that can be maintained and improved through individual, community, and professional efforts.

Serving the mentally ill requires major societal investment because of the relatively large number of persons afflicted and the cost of delivering treatment services. In many states, such activity represents the costliest item in the annual budget. In 1981, almost 1.5 million persons were added as admissions to specialty psychiatric services. At the same time, over several decades the use of psychotropic drugs has become a mainstay of policy to prevent hospitalization of the mentally impaired. There were 53 percent fewer psychiatric beds available in 1982 than in 1970. The number of outpatients added to the treatment rolls in 1981 was over 2,300,000 (excluding Veterans Administration medical centers). The outpatient and day treatment additions comprised 61 and 4 percent, respectively, of all additions of persons coming for treatment in 1981 as compared with 49 and 2 percent, respectively, in 1969.

Schizophrenia was the most frequent primary diagnosis for admission to state and county mental hospitals; affective disorders, for admission to private psychiatric hospitals; and alcohol-related disorders, for admission to VA medical centers.

Between 1970 and 1980, median days of stay for admissions to state and county medical hospitals decreased from 41 to 23 but remained relatively stable in private psychiatric hospitals and in nonfederal general hospitals.

In 1982, more than 390,000 full-time equivalent staff were employed in U.S. mental health organizations. Social workers were well represented in the professional staffing of these organizations.

The care of mentally retarded individuals represents a parallel system, most often under independent administration, to that providing care for those suffering from mental illness. Reflecting the national policy of reducing the number of mentally retarded in institutions, there was a decrease in the numbers of mentally retarded people living in state-operated residential facilities from 163,730 at the end of 1960 to 124,868 at the end of 1982—a decline of 23.7 percent. A different trend was evident in private institutions caring for the mentally retarded, which showed an increase from 89,120 patients at the end of 1977 to 115,032 at the end of 1982—an increase of 40.1 percent.

An allied area of interest with respect to national well-being concerns the abuse of alcohol and drugs. In the United States, the per capita rate of alcohol consumption rose approximately 21 percent in the 1960s, 10.3 percent during the 1970s, and 8.3 percent during the period from 1970 to 1982. Overall, between 1960 and 1982, the increase in the per capita rate of alcohol consumption was 31.9 percent. It is important to note that only 30 percent of the drinking population accounts for 80 percent of the total amount of alcohol consumed.

TABLE 8.1. RESIDENTIAL FACILITIES FOR THE MENTALLY RETARDED, 1960–1982

There has been a decline in use of institutions for the mentally retarded since 1970. Use of community facilities increased more than did the use of private facilities between 1977 and 1982.

Year	Number of Institutions	Resident Patients at End of Year	Total Admissions[a]	Net Releases
State Operated				
1960	108	163,730	14,701	6,451
1965	143	187,273	17,300	7,993
1970	190	186,743	14,985	14,702
1975	210	159,041	13,424	18,320
1978	398	152,476	14,286	19,665
1979	391	147,729	17,308	21,406
1980	394	140,230	14,064	16,225
1981	371	131,996	11,510	14,643
1982	364	124,868	10,111	13,479
Community Facilities				
1977	4,290	76,250	17,398	9,297
Private Facilities				
1977	10,219	89,120	22,363	12,384
1982	14,605	115,032	22,431	12,999

[a] Includes readmissions and excludes transfers.
Sources: *Statistical Abstract of the United States, 1982–83*, p. 117; and *Statistical Abstract of the United States, 1986*, p. 112.

TABLE 8.2. AVERAGE DAILY INPATIENT CENSUS BY TYPE OF MENTAL HEALTH ORGANIZATION, UNITED STATES, SELECTED YEARS 1969–1981

Drug therapy, deinstitutionalization, and federal cutbacks have contributed to a sharp decline in the censuses of state and county mental hospitals; the use of private and nonfederal psychiatric services continued to grow.

Type of Organization	1969	1975	1979	1981
All organizations	468,831	287,588	233,384	211,024
State and county mental hospitals	367,629	193,380	138,600	122,073
Private psychiatric hospitals	11,608	12,058	13,901	15,281
Nonfederal general hospital psychiatric services	17,808	22,874	23,110	29,307
VA psychiatric services	47,140	32,123	28,693	20,798
Federally funded CMHCs	5,270	10,186	9,886	—
RTCs for emotionally disturbed children	12,406	16,164	18,054	16,786
All other organizations	970	803	1,140	6,779

Source: *Mental Health United States, 1985*, p. 34.

TABLE 8.3. NUMBERS AND RATE OF ADMISSIONS TO PUBLIC AND PRIVATE PSYCHIATRIC SERVICES, BY RACE AND SEX, 1980 (CIVILIAN POPULATION)

Nonwhites are admitted to state and county inpatient psychiatric services at a rate more than twice that of whites; admission rates to private facilities do not differ substantially by race. Males show almost twice the rate of admission to state and county hospitals as do females; this holds across races.

Category	Numbers Admitted		Rate per 100,000	
	State and County	Private	State and County	Private
Total, all races	369,049	141,209	163.6	62.6
Male	239,400	67,395	219.8	61.9
Female	129,649	73,814	111.1	63.3
White	265,442	123,051	136.8	63.4
Male	171,341	58,074	182.2	61.7
Female	94,101	64,977	94.1	65.0
All other races	103,607	18,158	328.0	57.5
Male	68,059	9,321	457.8	62.7
Female	35,548	8,837	212.6	53.8

Source: U.S. National Institute of Mental Health, *Mental Health United States, 1985* (Washington, D.C.: U.S. Government Printing Office, 1985, DHHS Publication No. [ADM]85-1378), pp. 38–39.

TABLE 8.4. TRENDS IN NUMBER OF FULL-TIME EQUIVALENT (FTE) STAFF POSITIONS IN MENTAL HEALTH ORGANIZATIONS (EXCEPT VETERANS ADMINISTRATION), BY DISCIPLINE, 1976 AND 1982

Women predominate in the delivery of mental health services through their roles in nursing and social work. In six years the number of full-time equivalent staff positions in these two professions expanded considerably.

Staff Discipline	All Mental Health Organizations		Freestanding Outpatient Clinics	
	1976	1982	1976	1982
All staff	334,006	390,413	23,099	48,076
Patient care staff	226,530	271,224	16,706	32,800
Psychiatrist	11,576	13,586	1,449	1,952
Other physicians	2,551	2,802	76	119
Psychologists	9,453	16,600	3,704	6,093
Social workers	17,515	29,621	5,755	10,653
Registered nurses	29,478	43,450	830	2,162
Other health professionals	26,165	165,165	2,509	6,858
Physical health professionals	7,323	—	213	700
Other mental health workers	122,469	—	2,170	4,263
Administrative, clerical, and maintenance staff	107,476	119,189	6,393	15,276

Source: *Mental Health United States, 1985*, pp. 54, 58.

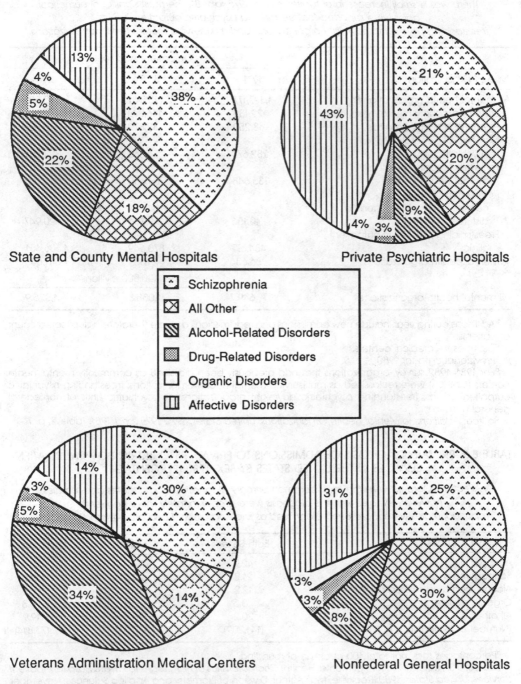

FIGURE 8.1. INPATIENT PSYCHIATRIC ADMISSIONS, BY DIAGNOSIS AND TYPE OF INSTITUTION, 1980

State and County Mental Hospitals

Private Psychiatric Hospitals

- Schizophrenia
- All Other
- Alcohol-Related Disorders
- Drug-Related Disorders
- Organic Disorders
- Affective Disorders

Veterans Administration Medical Centers

Nonfederal General Hospitals

Source: *Mental Health United States, 1985,* p. 19.

TABLE 8.5. OUTPATIENT SERVICE ADDITIONS TO MENTAL HEALTH ORGANIZATIONS BY TYPE OF ORGANIZATION, UNITED STATES, 1971, 1975, AND 1981[a]

There was a small increase in outpatients from 1975 to 1981. The most significant numerical gains were reported for freestanding psychiatric outpatient clinics, freestanding psychiatric day/night organizations, and multiservice mental health organizations.

Type of Organization	Outpatient Additions		
	1971	1975	1981
All mental health organizations[b]	1,327,177	2,195,844	2,335,510
State and county mental hospitals	129,133	146,078	73,265
Private psychiatric hospitals	18,250	32,879	69,660
Nonfederal general hospital psychiatric services	282,677	254,665	323,341[c,d]
Federally funded community mental health centers	335,648	784,638	—[d]
Residential treatment centers (RTCs) for emotionally disturbed children	10,156	19,784	20,947
Freestanding psychiatric outpatient clinics	484,677	870,649	1,306,451
Mental health organizations	66,636	87,151	541,846
	Rate per 100,000 civilians		
All mental health organizations[b]	649.7	1,038.8	1,025.9

[a]Additions during year include new admissions and readmissions and are therefore a duplicated count of patients.
[b]Excludes VA medical centers.
[c]Provisional data for 1980.
[d]For 1981–1982 survey, organizations that had previously been classified as community mental heath centers (CMHCs) were reclassified as multiservice mental health organizations, freestanding psychiatric outpatient clinics, freestanding psychiatric day/night organizations, or psychiatric units of nonfederal general hospitals.
Source: *Additions to Mental Health Organizations, United States, 1971, 1975, and 1981,* Table 2, p. 7.

TABLE 8.6. PRIMARY DIAGNOSIS OF ADMISSIONS TO PRIVATE PSYCHIATRIC HOSPITAL INPATIENT SERVICES IN THE UNITED STATES BY SEX, 1980 (PERCENTAGE)[a]

Affective disorders were the most common primary diagnosis for both males and females; however, females with this diagnosis were proportionately more frequently reported. Males were more often diagnosed as showing alcohol and drug-related problems.

Primary Diagnosis	Both Sexes	Male	Female
Affective disorders	42.9	34.2	50.8
Schizophrenia	21.2	23.2	19.5
Alcohol and drug-related disorders	12.2	18.3	6.6
Organic disorders	3.5	3.8	3.3
All other	20.2	20.5	19.9
(Number of patients)	(141,209)	(67,395)	(73,814)

[a]Percentages may not total 100 because of rounding.
Source: U.S. National Institute of Mental Health, *Characteristics of Admissions to Private Hospital Inpatient Services, United States, 1980* (Rockville, Md.: Author, Division of Biometry and Applied Sciences, November 1985), p. 5.

TABLE 8.7. DISTRIBUTION OF ADMISSIONS TO PRIVATE PSYCHIATRIC HOSPITAL INPATIENT
SERVICES, BY PRIMARY DIAGNOSIS, RACE, AND AGE, UNITED STATES, 1980
(PERCENTAGE)[a]

*Affective disorders are most common. Diagnoses of schizophrenia are found most
often in the 18–44 age groups, and organic disorders among
admissions 65 and over. Substantial racial differences are also apparent.*

Race and Primary Diagnosis	Total	Age				
		Under 18	18–24	25–44	45–64	65 and Over
All races	100.0	100.0	100.0	100.0	100.0	100.0
Affective disorders	42.9	29.7	32.7	43.6	51.1	54.0
Schizophrenia	21.2	12.6	33.2	25.2	16.3	6.7
Alcohol and drug-related disorders	12.2	4.5	9.6	13.8	16.7	9.2
Organic disorders	3.5	0.9	1.3	1.0	3.8	20.1
All other	20.2	52.3	23.2	16.4	12.1	10.1
White	100.0	100.0	100.0	100.0	100.0	100.0
Affective disorders	44.5	29.7	35.1	45.5	52.2	55.2
Schizophrenia	19.2	10.9	29.4	23.0	16.0	6.5
Alcohol and drug-related disorders	12.3	5.0	9.8	13.7	16.6	9.5
Organic disorders	3.4	0.8	1.2	0.9	3.4	18.7
All other	20.6	53.5	24.5	16.8	11.9	10.0
All other races	100.0	100.0	100.0	100.0	100.0	100.0
Affective disorders	31.5	29.1	19.5	33.4	40.0	39.2
Schizophrenia	35.0	25.2	54.1	37.0	20.1	9.2
Alcohol and drug-related disorders	11.6	1.0	8.5	14.0	18.3	5.7
Organic disorders	4.4	1.4	2.1	1.3	7.7	35.5
All other	17.5	43.4	15.8	14.3	13.9	10.4
(Number of patients)	(141,209)	(16,735)	(23,282)	(55,696)	(31,580)	(13,916)

[a]Percentages may not total 100 because of rounding.
Source: *Characteristics of Admissions to Private Hospital Inpatient Services, United States, 1980*, p. 11.

FIGURE 8.2. MEDIAN DAYS OF STAY, INPATIENT PSYCHIATRIC SERVICES, 1970–1980

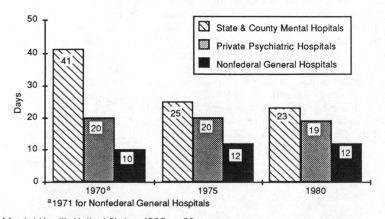

[a]1971 for Nonfederal General Hospitals

Source: *Mental Health United States, 1985*, p. 23.

SECTION 9. CHILD WELFARE

In 1985, there were 62.5 million children in the United States aged 18 years or under, living in 31.1 million family households. Infant mortality has been reduced, child crime rates have been going down, and there have been advances in educational attainment. Although a great majority of children lead healthy lives and are privileged compared to children in many other countries, certain subclasses remain highly vulnerable. The information provided here emphasizes the problematic conditions because there are substantial pockets of misery among children in the United States, and the failures of our society to provide adequately for them are of particular concern to professions oriented to rendering service. The size of groups of children living under conditions of blight must be charted over time to indicate whether our society is making progress.

Our choice of topics for this section was guided by one or more of the following criteria: (1) issues involving large numbers of children; (2) serious problems that place a heavy burden on children, their families, and their communities; (3) the availability of organized and reliable data; and (4) the response, through programs and service systems reflecting major societal investment. For example, in a single year almost half a million children experienced separation from their families requiring foster care arrangements. We report trend data showing that a national policy of permanency planning to prevent family breakup or sustained sojourns of children in foster care seems to be paying off. There are fewer children in care and, on the average, they are remaining in care for shorter periods. On the other hand, in 1984, official reporting of child abuse and neglect showed over a million families with 1,700,000 children. The number would be significantly higher if unreported cases were included. It is clear that black and other minority children are particularly afflicted. They are overrepresented in the foster care system and in

training schools for delinquent children. Such data reflect in part the widespread poverty characteristic of single-parent households. Yet there are areas where majority white children seem more afflicted. Teenage suicide has become an increasingly worrisome phenomenon, and white males show the greatest vulnerability in recent years. Similarly, the phenomenon of sexual molestation of children appears to be equally prevalent among both whites and minority groups.

The paucity of data and the poor quality of data-gathering efforts make it difficult to illuminate some important areas related to children's needs; for example, the last year in which there was well-organized information about the number and kinds of adoption taking place in the United States was 1975. The field of child welfare services has been particularly beset with problems of individual states refusing to participate in common data-gathering ventures despite a mandate in federal legislation. Noteworthy efforts have been made in some areas by the Administration for Children, Youth, and Families (Department of Health and Human Services) through contracts with research organizations and in its own intramural studies. Overall, however, fiscal support for the organization of routinely gathered data on a national level in various problem and service areas has been quite meager. Some of the slack has been taken up by advocacy organizations such as the Children's Defense Fund. With the growing availability of computers and major advances in information technology through sophisticated software, information gathering could be done relatively inexpensively—if there were a will to find out what is happening to the nation's children.

Topics not reflected in this section that merit inclusion in future editions of this volume include teenage pregnancy prevention programs, services funded under the Adoption Assistance and Child Welfare Act of 1980 (P.L. 96-272), community-based recreation services for children, and problems related to failure-to-thrive infants.

TABLE 9.1. TRENDS OF CHILDREN IN FOSTER CARE, 1980–1984

There has been a decline of 9 percent of children in foster care with much variation among states and regions. California shows an increase of 40 percent, and New York State shows a decrease of 36 percent.

Region	First Day 1980	First Day 1982	First Day 1983	First Day 1984	Last Day 1984	Trend 1980– 1984 (percent- age)
National Estimate	303,697	190,142	264,778	274,141	275,756	−9.2
Region 1 (Conn., Maine, Mass., N.H., R.I., Vt.)	19,466	19,378	18,531	18,408	17,612	−10.0
Region 2 (N.J., N.Y.)	51,037	36,039	39,661	35,311	33,022	−35.0
Region 3 (Del., D.C., Md., Pa., Va., W.Va.)	37,541	24,118	32,111	31,351	31,255	−17.0
Region 4 (Ala., Fla., Ga., Ky., Miss., N.C., S.C., Tenn.)	44,834	32,481	33,205	36,677	36,584	−18.0
Region 5 (Ill., Ind., Mich. Minn., Ohio, Wisc.)	64,298	27,835	55,314	58,961	58,697	−9.0
Region 6 (Ark., La., N.M. Okla., Texas)	16,753	15,735	16,855	15,853	17,501	4.0
Region 7 (Iowa, Kans., Mo., Neb.)	17,020	13,035	16,860	17,031	17,549	3.0
Region 8 (Colo., Mont., N.Dak., S.Dak., Utah, Wyo.)	8,083	5,940	7,186	7,578	7,329	−9.0
Region 9 (Ariz., Calif., Hawaii, Nev.)	31,264	2,549	32,687	38,880	42,464	36.0
Region 10 (Alaska, Idaho, Oreg., Wash.)	11,647	11,934	10,838	12,507	12,150	4.0

Source: U.S. Department of Health and Human Services, *Comparative Statistical Analysis of 1984 Child Welfare Data* (Washington, D.C.: U.S. Government Printing Office, 1986).

TABLE 9.2. DURATION OF PLACEMENT FOR CHILDREN[a] IN FOSTER CARE,
BY RACIAL AND ETHNIC GROUPS, 1982 (PERCENTAGE)

*Black children in foster care are more likely to experience extended
stays in care, lasting four years or more.*

Duration (in months)	White Not Hispanic	Black Not Hispanic	Hispanic	Asian or Pacific Islander	American Indian or Alaska Native
1–6	26.7	18.0	22.7	49.8	32.0
7–12	15.5	13.4	7.9	13.6	10.0
13–24	2.02	13.6	15.8	14.4	16.2
25–48	18.3	20.1	19.7	16.0	3.8
49–59	3.9	8.2	20.2	0.0	0.0
60 or more	13.8	26.4	11.8	6.3	38.0
Unknown	1.5	0.3	1.9	0.0	0.0
Total[b]	99.9	100.0	100.0	100.0	100.0
N	(157,950)	(61,722)	(12,393)	(2,916)	(7,776)
Percent	65.1	25.4	5.1	1.2	3.2

[a]Total number of children = 242,757.
[b]Some totals do not equal 100 percent because of rounding.
Source: U.S. Department of Health and Human Services, *National Child Welfare Indicator Survey*
(Washington, D.C.: U.S. Government Printing Office, December 1982).

FIGURE 9.1. LENGTH OF TIME IN FOSTER CARE PER CHILD, 1977–1983

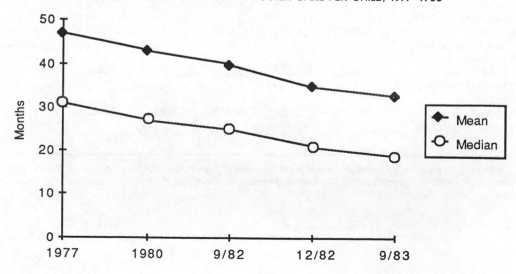

Source: Data from U.S. Department of Health and Human Services, *Comparative Statistical Analysis of
1983 State Child Welfare Data* (Washington, D.C.: Author, 1985), Vol. 1, p. G-10.

TABLE 9.3. PERCENTAGE OF SCHOOL ENROLLMENT SERVED AS HANDICAPPED, BY
HANDICAPPING CONDITION, 50 STATES AND THE DISTRICT OF COLUMBIA,
1976–1977, 1982–1983, AND 1983–1984[a]

The steady decline in the proportion of children counted as mentally retarded coincides with
increases in the learning-disabled and emotionally-disturbed categories. Physical
impairments have also decreased, indicating the impact of early diagnosis and treatment.
The total annual number of children receiving services has increased by over
1.4 million since the passage of the Education For All Handicapped Children Act in 1975.

Handicapping Condition	1976–1977	1982–1983	1983–1984
Learning disabled	1.79	4.40	4.57
Speech impaired	2.84	2.86	2.86
Mentally retarded	2.16	1.92	1.84
Emotionally disturbed	0.64	0.89	0.91
Other health impaired	0.32	0.13	0.13
Multihandicapped[b]	—	0.07	0.07
Hard of hearing/deaf	0.20	0.18	0.18
Orthopedically impaired	0.20	0.14	0.14
Visually handicapped	0.09	0.07	0.07
Deaf-blind[b]	—	0.01	0.01
Total	8.33	10.76	10.89
(Total number served)	(3,708,913)	(4,298,327)	(4,341,399)

[a]Percentages based on school enrollment for preschool through twelfth-grade children and handicapped enrollment for children aged 3 through 21.
[b]Data for these categories were not collected for 1976–1977.
Source: U.S. Department of Education, *Seventh Annual Report to Congress on the Implementation of
the Education for All Handicapped Children Act, 1985* (Washington, D.C.: U.S. Government Printing Office,
1985), p. 2.

TABLE 9.4. SUMMARY PROFILE FOR CASES OF REPORTED CHILD MALTREATMENT, 1984

The maltreatment of children occurs most often at the hand of parents.
It occurs among all racial and ethnic groups.

Category	Child	Caretaker	Perpetrator
Average age	7.29	31.9	31.5
Sex (percentage)			
Male	47.2	38.5	43.0
Female	52.8	61.5	57.0
Race (percentage)			
White	64.8	74.5	69.6
Black	19.9	17.5	19.1
Hispanic	12.4	5.5	9.3
Other	2.8	2.5	1.9
Perpetrator's relationship to child (percentage)			
Own child	84.6	—	—
Other relationship	6.2	—	—
Other	9.2	—	—

Source: *Highlights of Official Child Neglect and Abuse Reports, 1984*, pp. 21–23, 30.

TABLE 9.5. OFFICIAL REPORTS OF CHILD ABUSE AND NEGLECT REPORTING, TOTAL AND RATES BY STATES, DISTRICT OF COLUMBIA, AND TERRITORIES, 1984[a]

Over a million families were officially reported for child abuse and neglect. Reports have been rising in recent years and vary widely among states.
Six states accounted for more than four of every ten children reported.

| State | 1984 Reports | | Child Report Rates per 1,000 U.S. Children | | |
	Number of Families Reported	Number of Children Reported	1982	1983	1984
National	1,024,178	1,726,649	20.1	23.6	27.3
Alabama	18,303	28,407	21.24	21.04	25.59
Alaska	4,544	7,052	22.55	32.45	43.53
Arizona	12,749	19,788	—	—	23.12
Arkansas	12,558	20,974	23.34	25.89	32.17
California	138,061	250,271	33.71	35.24	37.57
Colorado	8,640	13,410	—	—	15.67
Connecticut	10,031	17,015	15.51	18.55	22.78
Delaware	3,811	7,887	—	52.66	50.88
District of Columbia	2,299	3,878	39.74	49.27	28.94
Florida	56,429	87,582	33.25	39.33	34.88
Georgia	21,359	36,229	18.61	21.70	22.20
Hawaii	2,877	3,971	10.78	11.21	13.84
Idaho	7,324	11,368	20.00	—	35.30
Illinois	39,233	67,058	19.58	20.55	21.70
Indiana	18,658	28,958	15.53	18.20	19.15
Iowa	15,804	25,018	28.14	29.52	31.95
Kansas	14,706	22,825	29.65	32.70	35.01
Kentucky	19,045	32,713	29.23	31.50	31.76
Louisiana	20,943	34,783	28.10	24.61	25.65
Maine	5,428	13,570	28.06	38.54	44.20
Maryland	5,204	8,077	—	13.30	7.44
Massachusetts	28,119	46,396	20.40	26.31	33.99
Michigan	41,352	90,627	32.10	34.33	36.45
Minnesota	14,109	23,673	12.63	14.36	21.08
Mississippi	4,487	6,964	—	—	8.74
Missouri	39,709	72,446	42.26	49.08	55.13
Montana	4,049	5,126	18.80	18.56	21.72
Nebraska	6,083	8,230	13.32	12.29	18.58
Nevada	6,066	8,795	36.07	32.01	37.59
New Hampshire	3,955	6,708	—	—	26.62
New Jersey	26,098	44,368	10.06	14.12	23.94
New Mexico	8,353	14,000	—	—	32.18
New York	81,093	134,699	—	21.72	30.69

(Continued on next page)

TABLE 9.5. (continued)

| State | 1984 Reports | | Child Report Rates per 1,000 U.S. Children | | |
	Number of Families Reported	Number of Children Reported	1982	1983	1984
North Carolina	17,970	26,201	16.84	17.00	16.38
North Dakota	2,856	4,431	19.37	19.32	22.38
Ohio	56,000	94,640	—	—	32.87
Oklahoma	11,693	18,149	16.66	16.50	19.71
Oregon	10,655	16,538	—	—	23.33
Pennsylvania	12,943	20,088	5.22	5.39	6.90
Rhode Island	5,470	8,490	—	—	37.57
South Carolina	14,125	23,958	25.45	16.75	25.84
South Dakota	6,536	10,145	25.24	27.34	49.25
Tennessee	20,531	41,063	25.83	29.70	32.98
Texas	64,313	105,882	20.21	21.35	22.45
Utah	8,945	14,967	—	—	23.95
Vermont	2,144	3,076	—	18.91	22.13
Virginia	27,603	42,842	28.23	30.09	30.00
Washinton	30,072	42,352	36.43	31.98	36.51
West Virginia	11,183	17,357	—	—	32.69
Wisconsin	11,083	17,202	6.90	7.46	13.47
Wyoming	2,346	3,502	16.30	20.30	21.89
Guam	390	580	—	—	—
Puerto Rico	5,526	11,831	—	—	—
Virgin Islands	225	349	—	—	—
Marianas Islands	90	140	—	—	—

[a]Twenty-five states reported estimates of either the number of families or the number of children based on a nationally derived ratio.

Source: American Association for Protecting Children, Inc., division of the American Humane Association, *Highlights of Official Child Neglect and Abuse Reports, 1984* (Denver, Colo.: Author, undated).

TABLE 9.6. NATIONAL ESTIMATE OF RATES AND NUMBERS OF CHILDREN REPORTED AS SEXUALLY MALTREATED, 1976–1984

Estimates of the number and rate of children who have experienced sexual molestation have shown a steady climb over the past decade. The number rose almost threefold between 1981 and 1984 alone.

Year	Estimated Number of Children in Thousands	Rate per 10,000 Children[a]	Percentage of U.S. Child Population From Which Rate Was Derived
1976	6	0.86	33
1977	11	1.74	36
1978	12	1.87	43
1979	27	4.23	42
1980	37	5.76	43
1981	35	5.55	47
1982	57	9.01	40
1983	74	11.86	46
1984	100	15.88	41

[a]The 95 percent confidence interval associated with this statistic is 13.77 to 21.61 per 10,000 children, and the error reflects state-level variability among 16 states. The range of variation is 4.9 to 37.4 per 10,000 children. The point estimate for the rate is the total number of children indicated as sexually maltreated divided by the under-18 population.

Source: *Highlights of Official Child Neglect and Abuse Reports, 1984*, p. 28.

FIGURE 9.2. CHILD ABUSE AND NEGLECT, BY TYPE OF MALTREATMENT, 1984

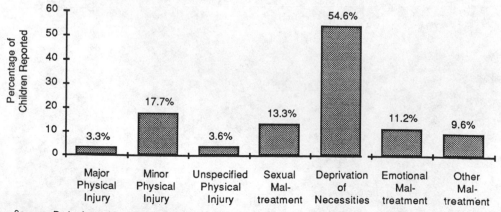

Source: Data from *Highlights of Official Child Neglect and Abuse Reports, 1984*, p. 5.

FIGURE 9.3. CHILD ABUSE AND NEGLECT REPORTS, NATIONAL ESTIMATES, 1976–1984

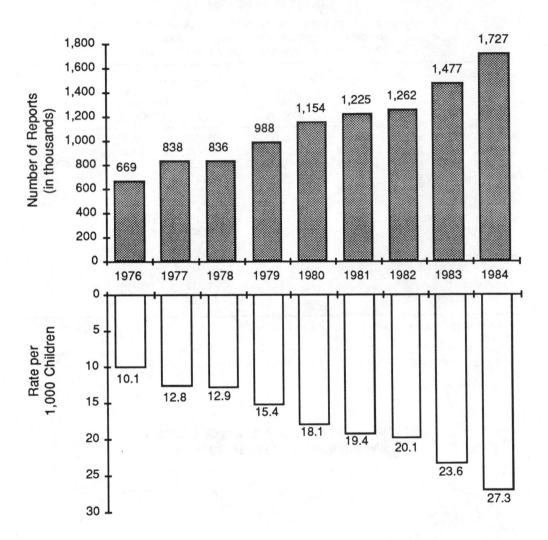

Source: Data from American Association for Protecting Children, Inc., *Highlights of Official Child Neglect and Abuse Reports, 1984* (Denver, Colo.: Author, undated), p. 5.

TABLE 9.7.   PUBLIC JUVENILE DETENTION AND TRAINING SCHOOL ADMISSIONS, ONE-DAY
COUNTS, 1971 AND 1982

*The admission rate to U.S. training schools increased by 5 percent in this period. The
female admissions rate declined by 41 percent,
and the male admissions rate increased by 18 percent.*

| | 1971 | | 1982 | | |
Category	Total	Rate Per 100,000	Total	Rate Per 100,000	Percentage Change[a] 1971–1982
Detention admissions	496,526	1,655	416,610	1,516	−8.4
Male	349,407	2,329	330,075	2,403	3.2
Female	147,119	981	86,535	630	−35.8
Detention, one-day count	11,767	39	13,048	47	20.5
Male	7,926	53	10,833	79	49.1
Female	3,841	26	2,215	16	−38.5
Training school admissions	67,775	226	65,401	238	5.3
Male	53,089	354	57,472	418	18.1
Female	14,686	98	7,929	58	−40.8
Training school, one-day count	35,960	120	25,071	91	−24.2
Male	27,874	186	22,213	162	−12.9
Female	8,086	54	2,858	21	−61.1
Eligible youth population	30,004,031		27,476,521		−8.4

[a]Percentage change denotes change in rate per 100,000 youth aged 10 to upper age of juvenile court
jurisdiction.
    Source: National Council on Crime and Delinquency and Hubert H. Humphrey Institute of Public Affairs,
Rethinking Juvenile Justice: National Statistical Trends (San Francisco, Calif.: Author, November 1984).

FIGURE 9.4. RACIAL COMPOSITION OF CHILDREN
IN JUVENILE TRAINING SCHOOLS, 1977 AND 1982

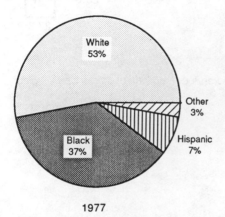
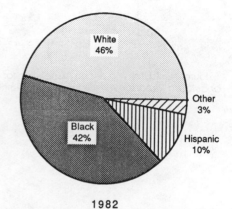

1977   1982

Source: Data from National Council on Crime and Delinquency and Hubert H. Humphrey Institute of
Public Affairs, *Rethinking Juvenile Justice: National Statistical Trends* (San Francisco: Author, 1984).

TABLE 9.8. CHILDREN ADOPTED IN THIRTY-THREE STATES BY AGE, 1983

Almost half the children are adopted before age 5. There is great variation among the regions, but because definitions are not uniform, caution must be observed in comparative analysis.

| Region | Age at Adoption (percentage) | | | | | Total Adopted (number) |
	Under 1	1–5	6–12	13–20	Unknown	
Total of reporting states	11.4	36.8	35.4	16.0	0.4	100.0 (13,980)
Region 1 (Conn., Maine, Mass., Vt.)	3.5	38.6	39.2	18.2	0.5	100.0 (990)
Region 2 (N.Y.)	0.9	34.5	41.7	21.8	1.1	100.0 (2,626)
Region 3 (Del., D.C., Pa., Va., W.Va.)	2.3	24.3	40.9	32.5	0.0	100.0 (2,004)
Region 4 (Ala., Fla., Ga., N.C., S.C., Tenn.)	6.4	47.7	33.7	11.6	0.6	100.0 (2,268)
Region 5 (Ind., Mich., Wisc.)	9.3	35.7	39.2	15.8	0.0	100.0 (1,349)
Region 6 (Ark., N.M., Texas)	11.0	46.9	30.8	11.1	0.2	100.0 (902)
Region 7 (Iowa, Kans., Mo., Neb.)	11.0	39.7	37.7	11.0	0.6	100.0 (965)
Region 8 (Colo., N.Dak., Wyo.)	22.3	31.5	33.1	13.1	0.0	100.0 (251)
Region 9 (Calif., Hawaii)	38.8	33.9	23.4	3.5	0.4	100.0 (1,959)
Region 10 (Oreg., Wash.)	29.7	37.8	24.8	7.7	0.0	100.0 (666)

Source: U.S. Department of Health and Human Services, *Child Welfare Statistical Fact Book, 1983 (Substitute Care, Adoption)* (Washington, D.C.: U.S. Government Printing Office, 1983), Table 29.

TABLE 9.9.   COMPARISON OF CHARACTERISTICS OF FOSTER CHILDREN FREE FOR ADOPTION WITH CHILDREN NOT FREE FOR ADOPTION, 1982[a]

Minority children and those not handicapped are more apt to be free for adoption. This is also true for children who are older and have been in foster care for extended periods. White and nonhandicapped children free for adoption are more likely to be in an adoptive placement. The same holds true for younger children and those who have been in foster care for shorter periods.

Characteristics	Free (percentage)	Not free (percentage)	Waiting Adoptive Placement (percentage)	Already in Adoptive Placement (percentage)
Total	21	79	66	34
(Number)	(50,000)	(193,000)	(33,000)	(17,000)
Race/ethnicity				
White	19	81	74	26
Minority	26	74	61	39
Handicap				
Handicapped	29	71	71	29
Not handicapped	37	63	63	37
Sex				
Female	22	78	64	36
Male	19	81	67	33
Age				
−1	35	65	54	46
1–3	23	77	46	54
4–6	22	78	53	47
7–10	21	79	55	45
11–14	20	80	69	31
15–18	17	83	92	8
Placement Duration				
0–6 months	11	89	71	29
7–12	9	91	60	40
13–24	13	87	64	36
25–48	28	72	57	43
49–59	41	59	78	22
60 or over	36	64	72	28

[a]Data obtained from the National Child Welfare Indicator Survey, December 1982, based on a national probability survey of 210 counties representing 81 percent of the sampled counties. Data were extracted from 4,063 case records of children less than 18 years of age who were in substitute care on December 15, 1982.

Source: *Child Welfare Research Notes #2* (December 1983).

SECTION 10. INTERNATIONAL COMPARATIVE DATA

Our purpose in this section is to provide enough information to enable American users of this volume to see some facets of our society in relation to others, in particular Japan, Canada, and the industrialized countries of Europe. Data presented here deal with demographic developments, health, employment, economic growth, and government activity in social welfare. The United States shares with these countries high levels of economic development and income; it differs in many ways in its responses to economic change and social need.

The British sociologist Peter Townsend[1] calculates that although in 1982 the United States ranked third of seven high-income countries in per capita GNP (behind Norway and Sweden), it ranks seventh in the share of GNP that goes to the poorest fifth of the population. In 1979, the share of all unemployed people in the United States who were out of work for six months or more was 8.8 percent, well below the level of other countries such as Canada (15.6 percent), the United Kingdom and West Germany (40 percent each), and Italy (55 percent). By 1983 the differences had narrowed substantially, although the U.S. share (24 percent) was still below that of the other countries. In part this difference reflects the broader coverage and higher support level of unemployment and other benefits in these countries compared to the United States. In the short run, more generous support for unemployed workers tends to extend job search time and thus to sustain the rate and duration of unemployment. Over the longer run, it has the effect of improving the match of job and job seeker, thereby improving economic performance.

In Section 7 we discussed the role of investor-owned corporations in health care delivery in the United States. Recent data show the increasing international involvement of the four major corporations most active in the health care field. The Hospital Corporation of America earned $10 million in profits from health-related activities in Australia, Brazil, Canada, Great Britain, India,

Malaysia, and Panama. Humana was smaller internationally in 1985 but expanding its activity rapidly; American Medical International owned extensive international properties involved in health care in Great Britain, Australia, Switzerland, and Spain. National Medical Enterprises was increasingly active in Japan, Britain, Singapore, and Malaysia. High-income and high-growth economies are attractive investment sites, as are markets in which high-technology medicine is well established. Even in Great Britain, with its national health service, private profit-making enclaves exist. Recent Conservative governments have welcomed and encouraged their expansion.

Data assembled by international organizations such as the Organization for Economic Cooperation and Development (OECD), the World Health Organization, the International Labor Office, and others make it possible to compare the United States with other countries regarding infant mortality, life expectancy, participation of women in the work force, male-female wage and salary ratios, and other indicators. Overall, the U.S. rankings are less impressive than they might be and are often discouraging. Although the number of physicians in the United States has increased substantially, the population per physician ratio is lower than in several countries, including Australia, Czechoslovakia, France, East and West Germany, Italy, the Netherlands, and the Soviet Union.

The most striking difference we find in comparing the United States and other industrialized countries—except Japan—is the magnitude and permanence of their commitment to social welfare expenditures even in times of economic difficulty (such as late 1970s and early 1980s). On the average, OECD countries devote larger shares of their social welfare expenditures to health care and unemployment compensation than does the United States. We have seen no persuasive evidence that this commitment explains or contributes to economic difficulties or that reduction in social welfare support would somehow transform stagnant economies into thriving ones; indeed, in our judgment the U.S. record after 1981 provides no support for this view. The causes appear to lie elsewhere and to exert their effect on all or most of the developed economies. For users of NASW publications this should be a source of reassurance and encouragement.

---

[1] P. Townsend. (1986). "Why Are the Many Poor?" *International Journal of Health Services,* 16 (1), 1–32.

TABLE 10.1. WORLD POPULATION BY REGION, 1970–1985

World population grew by 20 percent between 1970 and 1980, 9 percent between 1980 and 1985. Fifty-eight percent live in Asia, 5 percent in North America. Africa and Latin America have experienced rapid and continuous growth. East Asia, most notably China, has achieved a growth rate similar to that of industrialized areas.

Region	Midyear Population Estimates				
	Number (in thousands)			Average Annual Percentage Change	
	1970	1980	1985	1970–1980	1980–1985
World total	3,720,759	4,472,795	4,865,155	1.8	1.7
Africa	374,588	491,063	566,363	2.7	2.9
North America	226,483	251,922	264,147	1.1	.9
Latin America	285,690	364,254	409,589	2.4	2.3
Middle America	69,744	93,894	105,708	2.9	2.6
Caribbean	24,952	29,189	31,271	1.6	1.4
South America	190,994	242,171	272,610	2.4	2.4
East Asia	991,666	1,182,463	1,248,083	1.8	1.1
South Asia	1,120,303	1,410,526	1,583,141	2.3	2.3
Europe	459,976	484,412	491,987	.5	.3
Soviet Union	242,766	265,542	277,504	.9	.9
Oceania	19,286	22,612	24,340	1.6	1.5

Source: *Statistical Abstract of the United States, 1986,* p. 835.

TABLE 10.2. SELECTED DEMOGRAPHIC INDICATORS, 1982

Of these countries, the United States ranks first in divorces, first in marriages, second in births, lowest in births to unmarried women, and second lowest in its death rate.

Country	Birth-rate[a]	Death Rate[a]	Marriage Rate[a]	Divorce Rate[a]	Births to Unmarried Women Per 1,000 Live Births
Germany	10.1	11.6	5.9	1.9	84.9
France	14.6	10.0	5.7	—	126.8
Italy	10.9	9.4	5.5	0.2	45.9
Netherlands	12.0	8.2	5.8	2.2	58.7
Belgium	12.2	11.4	6.3	1.6	44.9
United Kingdom	12.8	11.8	6.9	2.8	141.0
Ireland	20.4	9.4	5.9	0.0	61.3
Denmark	10.3	10.8	4.8	2.9	382.7
United States	15.9	8.5	10.6	5.0	29.6

[a]Per 1,000 population.

Source: *Organization for Economic Cooperation and Development, Historical Statistics, 1960–1983* (Paris, France: Author, 1985), pp. 55, 107–108.

FIGURE 10.1. WORLD POPULATION, ANNUAL GROWTH RATE BY REGION, 1960–1985

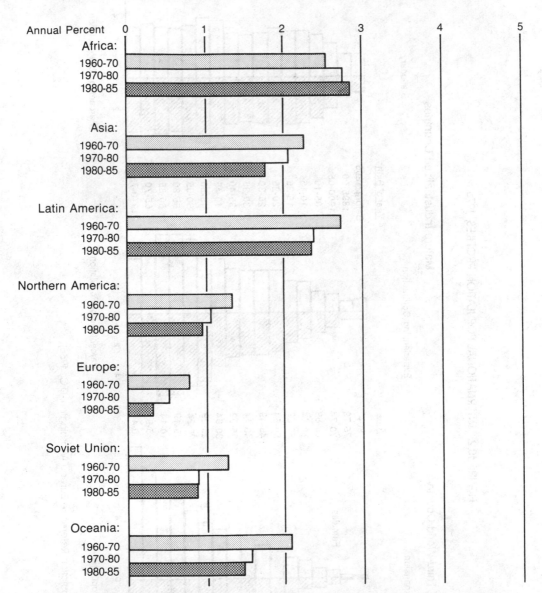

Source: U.S. Bureau of the Census, *World Population, 1985* (Washington, D.C.: Author, in press).

FIGURE 10.2   INTERNATIONAL POPULATION PROFILES, 1975

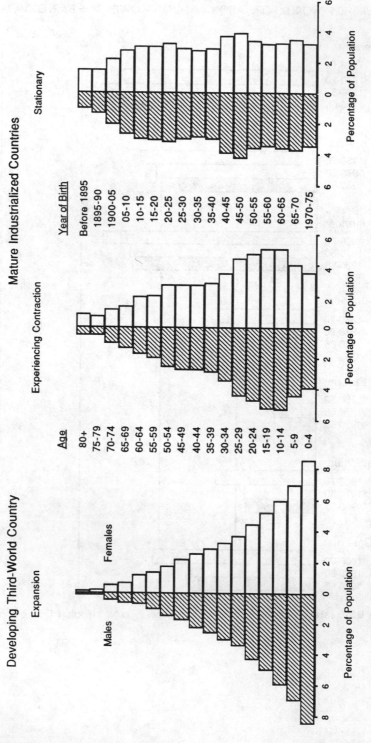

Source: Data from Population Reference Bureau (Washington, D.C., 1986).

TABLE 10.3. LIFE EXPECTANCY AT BIRTH, ACCORDING TO SEX, SELECTED COUNTRIES, SELECTED PERIODS, 1974–1981

Female-male differences are found in all countries shown. The United States ranks eighth of eighteen for females, twelfth (with France and Greece) for males.

Country	Female		Male	
	Period	Life Expectancy	Period	Life Expectancy
United States	1979	77.8	1979	70.1
Norway	1980–1981	79.2	1980–1981	72.7
Netherlands	1980	79.2	1980	72.5
Japan	1981	79.2	1981	73.8
Sweden	1981	79.1	1977–1978	72.0
Switzerland	1977–1978	78.7	1977–1978	72.4
Australia	1981	78.4	1981	71.4
France	1978–1980	78.2	1978–1980	70.1
Canada	1975–1977	77.5	1978–1980	70.4
Denmark	1980–1981	77.2	1980–1981	71.1
Germany	1979–1981	76.7	1979–1981	69.9
England and Wales	1978–1980	76.5	1978–1980	70.4
Austria	1980	76.2	1980	69.0
Italy	1974–1977	75.9	1974–1977	69.7
Israel	1981	75.9	1981	72.7
Poland	1981	75.2	—	—
Belgium	1972–1976	75.1	—	—
Cuba	1977–1978	74.9	1977–1978	71.5
Greece	—	—	1970	70.1
Ireland	—	—	1970–72	68.8

Source: *Health—United States, 1985,* p.45.

TABLE 10.4. INFANT MORTALITY RATES FOR SELECTED COUNTRIES, 1973 AND 1983

Infant mortality rates declined for all countries shown where data exists. The United States ranked eleventh of fifteen countries in 1973, twelfth in 1983.

Country	Rate per 1,000 Live Births		Average Annual Percentage Change 1977–1982
	1973	1983	
United States	17.7	11.2	−4.0
Australia	16.5	9.6	−5.4
Austria	23.9	11.9	−5.3
Canada	15.5	9.1	−6.2
Denmark	11.5	7.7	−0.7
England and Wales	16.9	10.1	−5.8
France	15.5	8.9	−4.2
German Democratic Republic[a]	15.6	12.3	−1.6
German Federal Republic	22.7	9.6[b]	−7.0
Ireland	18.0	9.8	—
Israel[a]	22.8	15.6	−3.8
Japan	11.8	6.2	—
Netherlands	11.5	8.3[b]	−3.1
Sweden	9.9	6.4[b]	−3.2
Switzerland	13.2	8.0	−6.2

[a]1982 data and percentage changes, *Health—United States, 1985,* p. 44.
[b] 1984.
Source: *Economic Surveys: United States, 1985/1986,* p. 143.

TABLE 10.5. LABOR FORCE AND UNEMPLOYMENT—SELECTED COUNTRIES, 1970–1984

The labor force grew most between 1980 and 1984 in the United States and Japan and slowly in the other countries shown. Unemployment rates were higher in all countries in the 1980s than in the 1970s. In 1970 and 1975 the U.S. and Canadian unemployment rates exceeded others. In 1984 several countries showed higher rates; significantly lower rates were shown for Japan and Sweden in both periods.

Country	Civilian Labor Force (in millions)					Percentage Unemployed				
	1970	1975	1980	1982	1984	1970	1975	1980	1982	1984
United States	82.8	93.8	106.9	110.2	113.5	4.9	8.5	7.1	9.7	7.5
Australia	5.5	6.2	6.7	6.9	7.1	1.6	4.9	6.1	7.2	9.0
Canada	8.4	10.0	11.6	12.0	12.4	5.7	6.9	7.5	11.0	11.3
Federal Republic of Germany[b]	26.2	26.1	26.5	26.6	26.7	.5	3.4	2.9	5.9	7.8
France	20.8	21.6	22.6	22.9	23.0[a]	2.5	4.2	6.4	8.4	10.1[a]
Great Britain	24.5	25.1	25.9	25.9	26.4[a]	3.0	4.5	6.8	11.8	13.0[a]
Italy	19.6	20.1	21.2	21.4	21.6[a]	2.8	3.0	3.9	4.8	5.6[a]
Japan	50.7	52.5	55.7	57.0	58.6	1.2	1.9	2.0	2.4	2.8
Sweden	3.9	4.1	4.3	4.4	4.4	1.5	1.6	2.0	3.1	3.1

[a]Preliminary estimates based on incomplete data.
[b]Federal Republic of Germany includes West Berlin.
Source: Statistical Abstract of the United States, 1986, p. 848.

TABLE 10.6. LABOR FORCE PARTICIPATION RATES, BY SEX, AND FEMALES AS PERCENTAGE OF TOTAL LABOR FORCE, SELECTED COUNTRIES, 1970–1984

Participation by women in the labor force rose in all countries shown except Japan, most markedly in Sweden, Canada, and the United States. Male participation rates were stable or declined. The share of women in the labor force was highest in Sweden in 1984; the United States ranked second.

| Country | Labor Force Participation Rates[a] | | | | | | Females as Percentage of Total Labor Force | | |
| | Female | | | Male | | | | | |
	1970	1980	1984	1970	1980	1984	1970	1980	1984
United States[b]	43.3	51.5	53.6	79.7	77.4	76.4	37.2	42.0	43.3
Canada	43.2	57.2	62.0	85.7	86.3	85.9	33.3	40.0	42.2
Federal Republic of Germany	48.1	50.0	49.4	92.5	83.4	79.1	35.9	38.1	38.5
France	47.5	52.5	56.1	87.8	82.5	77.2	35.4	40.1	42.5
Italy	33.5	39.8	—	86.8	82.9	—	26.8	33.4	—
Japan	55.4	54.9	57.2	89.4	89.0	88.4	39.3	38.7	39.6
Sweden	59.4	74.1	78.8	88.8	87.8	87.2	39.5	45.2	46.9
United Kingdom	50.8	58.7	59.9	94.3	90.8	86.1	35.3	39.5	41.2

[a]Labor force of all ages as percentage of population, 15–64 years old.
[b]Civilian labor force.
Sources: *Statistical Abstract of the United States,* 1986, pp. 392, 848; Organization for Economic Cooperation and Development, *Historical Statistics 1960–1982;* and *Labour Force Statistics,* annual (Paris, France: Author).

TABLE 10.7. CONSUMER PRICES, INCREASE OVER PREVIOUS YEAR (PERCENTAGE), 1965–1984

Inflation rates rose in all countries shown in the 1975–1980 period, declined sharply in some countries after 1980, and remained high in others, notably Italy, Greece, Portugal, and Spain.

Country	1965	1970	1975	1980	1981	1982	1983	1984
United States	1.7	5.9	9.1	13.5	10.4	6.1	3.2	4.3
Japan	6.6	7.7	11.8	8.0	4.9	2.7	1.9	2.2
Germany	3.4	3.4	6.0	5.5	6.3	5.3	3.3	2.4
France	2.5	5.2	11.8	13.6	13.4	11.8	9.6	7.4
United Kingdom	4.8	6.4	24.2	18.0	11.9	8.6	4.6	5.0
Italy	4.6	5.0	17.0	21.2	17.8	16.6	14.6	10.8
Canada	2.5	3.4	10.8	10.2	12.5	10.8	5.9	4.3
Austria	5.0	4.4	8.4	6.4	6.8	5.4	3.3	5.6
Belgium	4.1	3.9	12.8	6.6	7.6	8.7	7.7	6.3
Denmark	6.5	5.8	9.6	12.3	11.7	10.1	6.9	6.3
Greece	3.0	3.2	13.4	24.9	24.5	21.0	20.2	8.5
Ireland	5.0	8.2	20.9	18.2	20.4	17.1	10.5	8.6
Netherlands	4.0	3.6	10.2	6.5	6.7	6.0	2.8	3.3
Norway	4.3	10.6	11.7	10.9	13.6	11.3	8.4	6.2
Portugal	3.4	6.3	20.4	16.6	20.0	22.4	25.5	29.3
Spain	13.2	5.7	16.9	15.5	14.6	14.4	12.1	11.3
Sweden	5.0	7.0	9.8	13.7	12.1	8.6	8.9	8.0
Switzerland	3.4	3.6	6.7	4.0	6.5	5.6	3.0	2.9
Total OECD Countries	3.0	5.6	11.3	12.9	10.5	7.8	5.2	5.3

Source: Organization for Economic Cooperation and Development, *Economic Outlook* (Paris, France: Author, December 1985).

TABLE 10.8. GNP PER CAPITA, 1980–1983

Slow or negative growth was characteristic of most countries in the early 1980s.

Country	GNP per Capita in Constant (1983) Dollars		Annual Percentage Change 1980–1983
	1980	1983	
United States	13,941	14,093	.3
OECD Europe	7,184	7,213	.1
Belgium	8,213	8,245	.1
Denmark	10,059	10,684	2.0
Federal Republic of Germany	10,627	10,672	.1
France	9,393	9,473	.3
Greece	3,703	3,624	−.7
Ireland	4,706	4,729	.1
Italy	6,281	6,149	−.7
Netherlands	9,434	9,164	−.9
United Kingdom	7,691	7,999	1.3
Austria	8,596	8,848	.9
Finland	9,079	9,568	1.8
Iceland	10,000	9,167	−2.7
Norway	12,689	12,930	.6
Spain	3,994	4,057	.5
Sweden	10,542	10,744	.6
Switzerland	15,822	15,633	−.4
Turkey	995	1,078	2.7
Canada	12,762	12,662	−.2
Japan	8,956	9,697	2.7
New Zealand	6,688	6,813	.6

Source: *Statistical Abstract of the United States, 1986,* p. 843.

TABLE 10.9. TOTAL TAX REVENUE AS PERCENTAGE OF GROSS DOMESTIC PRODUCT AT MARKET PRICES, 1975 AND 1983

Except for Japan, the United States ranked lowest in total tax burden in both years shown, well below OECD average.

Country	1975	1983
Sweden	43.9	50.5
Netherlands	43.6	47.3
Norway	44.8	46.6
Denmark	41.4	46.2
Belgium	41.1	45.4
France	37.4	44.6
Italy	29.0	40.6
United Kingdom	35.5	37.8
Germany	36.0	37.4
Canada	32.9	33.0
Switzerland	29.6	31.6
Australia	29.1	30.0
United States	29.6	29.0
Japan	21.0	27.7
OECD total	32.9	37.0
EEC (Common Market)	35.7	41.4

Source: Organization for Economic Cooperation and Development, *Revenue Statistics of OECD Member Countries, 1965–1984* (Paris, France: Author, 1985), pp. 82–83.

TABLE 10.10. TAXES BY SOURCE AS PERCENTAGE OF TOTAL TAXATION, 1983

The U.S. overall tax level was comparatively low, relying less on sales and excise taxes and more on corporate and direct income taxes than other countries. Denmark and Australia levy the highest personal income taxes, France the highest social security taxes, Japan the highest corporate income taxes, and France and Canada the highest sales and excise taxes.

Country	Source		
	Personal Income	Corporte Income and Profits	Payroll and Workforce
Sweden	38.91	3.4	4.25
Netherlands	21.34	6.1	—
Norway	25.29	14.6	—
Denmark	52.01	3.0	—
Belgium	34.96	6.1	—
France	13.41	4.3	2.42
Italy	27.91	9.3	—
United Kingdom	27.70	10.8	1.36
Germany	28.26	5.1	—
Canada	35.58	7.5	—
Switzerland	35.61	6.0	—
Australia	43.94	8.8	5.83
United States	37.12	5.5	—
Japan	25.57	19.6	—
OECD total	32.32	6.9	1.14
EEC (Common Market)	27.54	6.9	0.73

Source: *Revenue Statistics of OECD Member Countries, 1965–1984*, pp. 86–87, 92.

TABLE 10.11. SOCIAL EXPENDITURES AS PERCENTAGE OF GROSS DOMESTIC PRODUCT IN 19 COUNTRIES, 1960–1981

The United States ranks fourteenth of the 19 countries listed here in its social expenditures.

Country	Social Expenditure Percentage of GDP	Real Social Expenditure Share		Annual Growth Rate of Real Social Expenditure		Decrease in the Annual Growth Rate Between 1960–1975 and 1975–1981	
						Real GDP	Real Social Expenditure
	1981	1960	1981	1960–1975	1975–1980	(Percentage)	
Belgium	37.6	17.2	35.0[a]	9.1	4.4[a]	2.3	1.4
Netherlands	36.1	18.0	33.9	9.3	1.4	2.5	8.8
Sweden	33.4	15.9	33.5	8.0	4.0	3.0	3.2
Denmark	33.3	—	31.8[b]	—	4.0	1.5	—
Germany	31.5	20.4	29.2	6.7	1.9	0.8	4.6
France	29.5	13.4[c]	29.1	7.5[c]	5.9	2.2	1.1
Italy	29.1	18.12	6.2	7.0	3.8	1.4	2.6
Ireland	28.4	12.5	25.1	8.2	6.0	0.8	2.0
Austria	27.7	19.2	25.9	6.0	4.4	1.6	2.7
Norway	27.1	12.1	27.1	9.5	5.6	0.2	5.5
Finland	25.9	15.8	26.0	7.4	4.5	1.6	−2.7
United Kingdom	23.7	14.8	23.1	5.0	2.5	1.6	4.1
Canada	21.5	12.3	22.1	9.5	2.7	1.8	6.2
United States	20.8	—	—	—	—	0.2	4.8
New Zealand	19.6	14.3	18.6	4.4	3.7	9.3	1.4
Australia	18.8	10.9	17.6	8.6	2.3	2.8	7.2
Japan	17.5	10.2	13.7	9.7	7.3	3.9	4.4
Switzerland	14.9	8.0	13.9	6.9[b]	2.5[b]	1.7	4.9
Greece	13.4	8.9	13.1	8.1[d]	8.8	3.3	−1.0[d]

[a]1980.
[b]1979.
[c]Excluding education.
[d]Indicating increase.

Source: *Organization for Economic Cooperation and Development, Social Expenditures 1960–1990,* (Paris, France: Author, 1985), pp. 21, 22.

TABLE 10.12 GOVERNMENT DEBT IN RELATION TO GROSS DOMESTIC PRODUCT (GDP)

The U.S. ratio is well below that of some EEC countries and above that of others. It rose faster than the EEC average and than most countries shown between 1980 and 1983.

Country	Government Debt as Percentage of GDP			
	1980	1981	1982	1983 (est.)
Belgium	9.4	12.6	11.9	12.2
Denmark	5.9	7.0	9.1	8.8
West Germany	3.5	3.9	3.5	3.3
Greece	0.4	10.1	6.4	6.3
France	—	1.8	2.7	3.1
Ireland	12.8	15.8	16.2	13.4
Italy	8.4	11.7	11.9	11.9
Luxembourg	1.8	2.3	2.0	2.9
Netherlands	3.4	5.2	6.9	6.7
United Kingdom	3.5	2.9	2.1	2.2
United States	2.3	2.0	3.6	6.1
EEC (Common Market) average	3.5	5.2	5.2	5.4

Source: *Socioeconomic Newsletter,* April–May, 1984.

FIGURE 10.3. MILITARY EXPENDITURES AND PRODUCTIVITY, 1960–1983

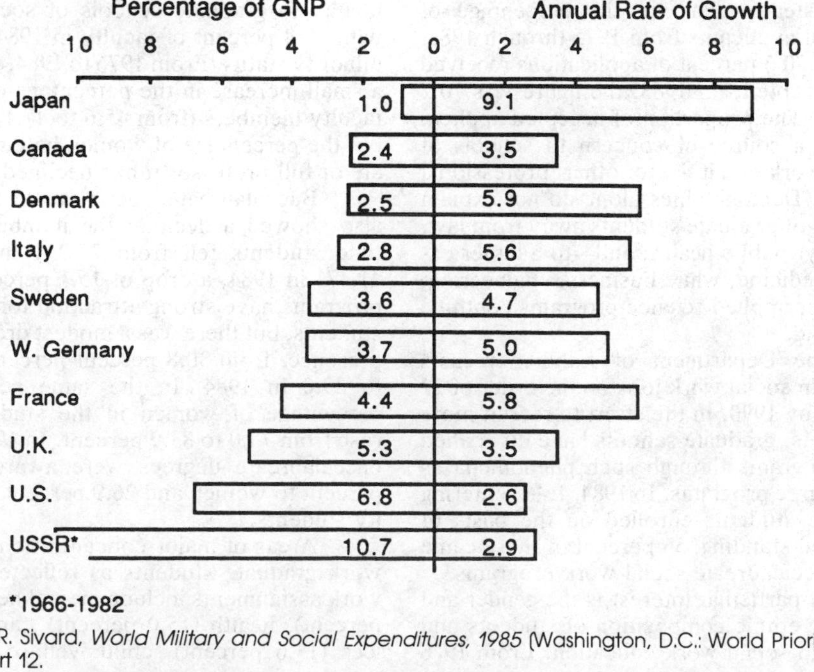

	Military Expenditures as Percentage of GNP	Manufacturing Productivity Annual Rate of Growth
Japan	1.0	9.1
Canada	2.4	3.5
Denmark	2.5	5.9
Italy	2.8	5.6
Sweden	3.6	4.7
W. Germany	3.7	5.0
France	4.4	5.8
U.K.	5.3	3.5
U.S.	6.8	2.6
USSR*	10.7	2.9

*1966-1982

Source: R. Sivard, *World Military and Social Expenditures, 1985* (Washington, D.C.: World Priorities, Inc., 1986), Chart 12.

SECTION 11. SOCIAL WORK EDUCATION

Enrollment of students in graduate social work programs seeking master's degrees and doctorates showed a fairly steep climb through the 1960s and well into the 1970s, reflecting the fact that social programs and social work education fared well in securing public funding during the Kennedy-Johnson years. The momentum was sufficient to carry continued support for social work training into the administrations of Nixon, Ford, and Carter.

After expanding every year from 1955 onward, a decline in the number of full-time students in master's programs occurred in 1979 and continued until 1984. There was a 17 percent drop in students from 1980 to 1984. Recent indications are that the current enrollment is being maintained despite the fact that the Reagan Administration has moved strongly to curtail grants for social programs and training grants, normally a major source of growth for social work education.

Data indicate that graduate schools have responded to the decline in applications for admission to first-year status by increasing the number of applicants accepted. There was a steady climb in the percentage of accepted applicants from 1975 through 1983. In 1982, 70.5 percent of applications received were accepted; for 1983, the figure was 70.2 percent. The proportion of accepted applications is a source of concern to schools of social work as it is to other professional schools. Demographics alone do not explain the shift of graduate students away from law, dentistry, public health, and—to a lesser extent—medicine, while business, engineering, and other applied science programs continue to expand.

The Department of Labor forecasts growth in social work jobs on the order of 22 percent by 1990. In the effort to recruit more applicants, graduate schools have diversified their programs through such phenomena as joint degree programs. In 1984, 1,463 entering graduate students enrolled on the basis of advanced standing; 56 percent of these came from baccalaureate social work programs.

Of particular interest is the gender and racial or ethnic composition of students and faculty in social work education. From 1976 to 1984, women as a percentage of full-time MSW students increased from 69.7 to 78.9 percent. They constituted 67.6 percent of those awarded degrees in 1976, and their proportion climbed 78.9 percent in 1984. The further increase in majority status of women in such a short time span is striking and consistent with aggregate data showing that many women continue to enter female-intensive occupations.

Minority composition among social work graduate students showed some decline. In 1976, 18.3 percent of the graduate students were of minority background; by 1984 this figure had declined to 16.2 percent. The award of MSW degrees showed a more pronounced trend, with 17.0 percent of those awarded degrees in 1976 being minority students; in 1984, the figure was down to 13.9 percent. Schools of social work have made a major investment in financial grants to minority students. The provision of financial aid to 80.6 percent of black, 84.8 percent of American Indian, 76.3 percent of Puerto Rican, and 65.2 percent of Hispanic students in 1984 helped to sustain the presence of minority students in graduate schools of social work.

On a more positive note, recent trends show an increase in the presence of minority faculty in graduate schools of social work, with 22.4 percent of faculty in 1984 being of minority status. From 1976 to 1984, there was a small increase in the percentage of women faculty members (from 45.6 to 47.1 percent), but the percentage of women holding associate or full professor ranks declined.

Baccalaureate social work education also showed a decline; the number of full-time students fell from 25,281 in 1976 to 21,471 in 1984, a drop of 15.1 percent. Such programs have strong attraction for minority students, but there was a modest drop in their presence, from 30.8 percent percent in 1976 to 29.0 in 1984. In the same period, the percentage of women in the student body rose from 75.0 to 83.9 percent. In 1984, 6,932 baccalaureate degrees were awarded, 86.7 percent to women and 26.9 percent to minority students.

Areas of major concentration of social work graduate students as reflected in field work assignments include mental health (24.2 percent), health (15.0 percent), family services (13.6 percent), child welfare (9.1 percent), and gerontological social work (5.1 percent). Together, these fields account for two-thirds of student field placements.

Labor Department occupational studies about social work are quite skimpy, and more needs to be learned about employment and salary trends in the profession. As yet, NASW has not completed canvassing its members about the jobs they hold and their income and job satisfaction. Planning is under way for creating a richer database to document how professional social workers are faring. Future issues of this statistical report will monitor trends that reflect an increased social work presence in important fields of practice. Such information, if broadly disseminated, has potential for securing new recruits to the profession; for example, through agency-based mental health services and through private practice, social workers are becoming a major source of psychotherapeutic treatment for the public.

A social work presence in health settings, such as hospitals and clinics, and in trade union and corporate settings is also manifesting increased strength. With the "graying of America," gerontological social work services are becoming more visible. The deinstitutionalization of mental patients and the general problem of homelessness are sectors in which social work skills in social planning, administration, and practice are being called on. There is reason to be optimistic that despite the decline in numbers of applicants to graduate schools, the profession will be well rooted in many service sectors.

TABLE 11.1. RECENT TRENDS IN GRADUATE SOCIAL WORK EDUCATION, 1976–1984

Women continue to increase their majority status in holding the MSW degree; minority MSW graduates are declining. After a marked increase in the number of full-time doctoral students in 1982, there was a precipitous drop in 1984. Degrees awarded also showed a drop after a previous steady climb. Women have become the majority among those awarded doctoral degrees, and minority students have constituted about a fifth of the degree holders.

Program and Student Category	1976	1978	1980	1982	1984
Master's degree programs					
Full-time students	16,869	17,672	17,122	15,131	14,275
Women (percentage)	69.7	72.2	75.8	79.2	80.4
Ethnic minority (percentage)	18.3	17.5	17.6	16.8	16.2
Master's degrees awarded	9,080	9,476	9,850	9,556	8,053[a]
Women (percentage)	67.6	72.1	73.5	78.6	78.9
Ethnic minority (percentage)	17.0	16.3	15.9	14.1	13.9
Doctoral degree programs					
Full-time students	769	821	825	922	798[a]
Women (percentage)	50.1	55.2	56.5	57.0	61.2
Ethnic minority (percentage)	23.8	23.6	19.7	21.6	21.9
Degrees awarded	179	178	213	284	245[a]
Women (percentage)	43.0	47.8	48.8	56.3	60.4
Ethnic minority (percentage)	20.1	14.0	20.7	17.4	21.5

[a]Response rate less than 100 percent.

Sources: A. Rubin, *Statistics on Social Work Education in the United States* (Washington, D.C.: Council on Social Work Education, 1985), p. 50; and Council on Social Work Education, *Statistics on Social Work Education in the United States: 1980* (New York, N.Y.: Author, 1981), Table 39.

FIGURE 11.1. ENROLLMENTS AND DEGREES AWARDED, GRADUATE SOCIAL WORK PROGRAMS, 1959–1984

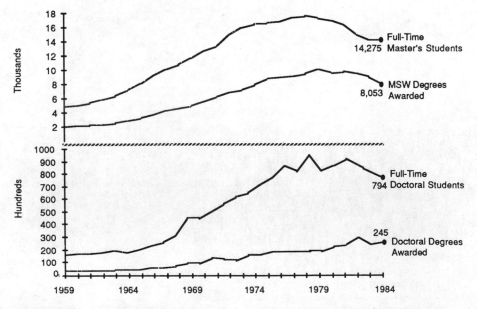

Sources: Data from A. Rubin, *Statistics on Social Work Education in the United States* (Washington, D.C.: Council on Social Work Education, 1984), p. 38; and Council on Social Work Education, *Statistics on Social Work Education in the United States: 1984* (Washington, D.C.: Author, 1985), p. 35.

TABLE 11.2 RECENT TRENDS IN GRADUATE SOCIAL WORK PROGRAMS, 1976–1984

The proportion of minority faculty increased across all ranks. The proportion of female faculty declined
for full-time professors, was static for associate professors,
and increased for assistant professors. Despite an apparent decline in the total number
of faculty positions, doctoral programs increased 50 percent in less than 10 years.

Category	1976	1978	1980	1982	1984
Schools					
Accredited master's					
degree programs	82	84	84	87	88
Doctoral programs	33	35	37	44	51
Faculty					
Total number	3,318	3,580	3,440[a]	2,967[a]	2,953[a]
Women (percentage)	45.6	47.7	47.4	47.1	47.1
Ethnic minority (percentage)	20.6	20.3	20.6	22.4	22.4
Full-time professors					
Women (percentage)	29.5	28.0	26.6	25.5	25.5
Ethnic minority (percentage)	10.9	13.8	16.0	16.1	18.0
Full-time associate professors					
Women (percentage)	42.1	40.8	38.7	40.8	40.7
Ethnic minority (percentage)	21.5	23.0	24.6	23.4	25.7
Full-time assistant professors					
Women (percentage)	51.5	55.1	55.6	59.8	60.4
Ethnic minority (percentage)	31.0	30.9	31.2	30.8	32.5

[a]Response rate less than 100 percent.
Sources: *Statistics on Social Work Education in the Unites States,* p. 50; and *Statistics on Social Work Education in the United States: 1980,* Table 39.

TABLE 11.3. RECENT TRENDS IN BACCALAUREATE SOCIAL WORK EDUCATION, 1976–1984

The growth of undergraduate programs has abated somewhat after rapid expansion in
the late 1970s and early 1980s. The presence of women is stronger
here among both students and faculty than in graduate social work programs. This
is also true, but to a lesser extent, for ethnic minority groups.

Category	1976	1978	1980	1982	1984
Accredited BSW Programs					
BSW only	143	181	214	269	288
Joint	38	46	47	54	55
Faculty (baccalaureate only)					
Total number	978	1,297	1,262	1,110	1,193[a]
Women (percentage)	46.8	50.4	51.8	50.2	54.1
Ethnic minority (percentage)	23.8	25.7	23.6	23.3	26.5
Students					
Full-time degree students	25,281	29,350	27,051	21,918	21,471[a]
Women (percentage)	75.0	81.1	84.7	85.0	83.9
Ethnic minority (percentage)	30.8	31.0	30.0	28.7	29.0
Degrees awarded	7,102	9,277	7,971	7,802	6,392[a]
Women (percentage)	77.1	77.7	84.2	85.9	86.7
Ethnic minority (percentage)	23.1	25.4	26.3	24.0	26.9

[a]Response rate less than 100 percent.
Sources: *Statistics on Social Work Education in the United States,* p. 50; and *Statistics on Social Work Education in the United States: 1980,* Table 39.

TABLE 11.4. PROFESSIONAL SCHOOL APPLICATIONS AND FIRST-YEAR ENROLLMENT TRENDS, 1977–1984

Both applications and enrollments declined in these professional institutions. Other areas of graduate education—business, engineering, communications, and so on—did not.

Year	Law		Dentistry		Medicine		Social Work		Public Health[c]		Nursing[d]	
	Applied[a]	Enrolled	Applied	Enrolled	Applied	Enrolled	Applied	Enrolled[b]	Applied	Enrolled	Applied	Enrolled
1977	—	39,676	81,765	5,954	371,545	16,134	—	17,533	12,326	—	83,119	37,348
1978	—	40,479	66,585	6,301	335,982	16,620	—	17,672	13,000	23,391	69,390	35,611
1979	—	40,717	58,715	6,132	335,217	17,014	30,954[c]	17,397	—	—	80,099	35,414
1980	70,999	42,296	52,218	6,030	330,888	17,204	28,852	17,122	11,898	—	67,144	35,808
1981	72,911	42,521	46,894	5,855	339,975	17,320	26,349	16,552	11,078	—	62,947	35,928
1982	71,755	42,034	41,466	5,498	334,897	17,230	20,786	15,131	10,021	2,852	67,999	—
1983	64,100	41,159	38,004	5,274	319,340	17,175	20,780[c]	14,265	9,998	2,825	—	—
1984	60,133	40,747	35,413	5,047	—	16,997	—	—	—	—	—	—

[a] Law figures are for applicants only; each applicant averaged 4.18 applications in 1984, 4.3 in 1982.
[b] Total students enrolled in MSW programs.
[c] Response rate slightly less than 100 percent.
[d] Nursing figures are for baccalaureate programs only.
Source: S. Watson, A. Meyer, & S. Wotman, "The Demand for Professional Education: A Growing Crisis for the Public Health and Public Welfare?" *Journal of Dental Education* (in press).

TABLE 11.5. MASTER'S DEGREE STUDENTS ENROLLED, BY PRIMARY CONCENTRATION, NOVEMBER 1, 1984

Mental health, followed by health and family services, was the most frequently chosen field of concentration in 1984.

Concentration	Number	Percent-age
Gerontological social work	529	5.1
Alcohol, drug, or substance abuse	248	2.4
Child welfare	941	9.1
Community planning	297	2.9
Corrections/criminal justice	263	2.5
Family services	1,403	13.6
Group services	122	1.2
Health	1,544	15.0
Industrial social work	181	1.8
Mental health or community mental health	2,496	24.2
Mental retardation	146	1.4
Public assistance/public welfare	222	2.2
Rehabilitation	103	1.0
School social work	333	3.2
Other field of practice or social problem	1,064	10.3
Combinations	431	4.2
Not yet determined	4,625	—
None (methods concentration only)	6,621	—
Total	21,569	100.0

Source: *Statistics on Social Work Education in the United States*, p. 43.

TABLE 11.6. EMPLOYMENT OF SOCIAL WORKERS IN 1984

The vast majority of social workers are wage and salary employees. Over two-fifths are employed by the government, and one-fifth work in health-related facilities. Less than 2 percent are in private practice.

Category	Social Workers Number	Social Workers Percent
Total	335,465	100.0
Wage and salary	329,465	98.2
Self-employed	6,000	1.8
Nursing and personal care facilities	5,096	1.5
Hospitals	36,260	11.0
Outpatient care facilities	21,818	6.6
Educational services	15,959	4.8
Individual and family social services	33,964	10.3
Job training and vocational rehabilitation	6,860	2.0
Residential care	12,309	3.7
Social services N.E.C.[a]	255,270	7.7
Civil, social, and fraternal associations	9,205	2.8
Religious organizations	6,775	2.1
Federal government	4,569	1.4
State government	76,761	23.3
Local government	64,433	19.6

[a]Not elsewhere classified.

Source: U.S. Department of Labor, unpublished data (Washington, D.C.: 1985).

FIGURE 11.2 SOCIAL WORK EMPLOYMENT, 1984[a]

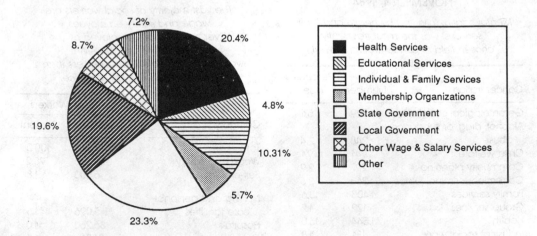

ᵃExcluding federal hospitals and self-employment.

Source: Data from U.S. Department of Labor, Bureau of Labor Statistics, unpublished tables (Washington, D.C., 1986).